The style of the short poem

The style of the short poem

James McMichael
University of California, Irvine

Wadsworth Publishing Company, Inc.
Belmont, California

acknowledgments

Holt, Rinehart and Winston, Inc.—for "The Most of It" from *Complete Poems of Robert Frost*. Copyright 1942 by Robert Frost. Reprinted by permission of Holt, Rinehart and Winston, Inc.

The Macmillan Company—for "During Wind and Rain" by Thomas Hardy from *Collected Poems*. Copyright 1925 by The Macmillan Company. Reprinted with permission.

The Macmillan Company of Canada Limited—for "During Wind and Rain" from *Collected Poems of Thomas Hardy* by permission of The Estate of Thomas Hardy, Macmillan & Co., Ltd., London, and the Macmillan Company of Canada Limited.

New Directions Publishing Corporation—for "This Is Just to Say" and "Blueflags" from *The Collected Earlier Poems of William Carlos Williams*. Copyright 1938 by William Carlos Williams. Reprinted by permission of New Directions Publishing Corporation.

Robert Pinsky—for his "Old Woman."

The Southern Review—for "Old Woman" by Robert Pinsky, which first appeared in *The Southern Review*. Copyright 1965 by Robert Pinsky. Reprinted by permission.

Alan Swallow, Publisher—for "In Whose Will Is Our Peace?" by J. V. Cunningham. Reprinted from *The Exclusions of a Rhyme: Poems and Epigrams* by J. V. Cunningham. Copyright 1960 by J. V. Cunningham. By permission of the publisher.

Wadsworth Publishing Company, Inc.—"The Last Distances" and "Thinking of the Oregon Rains" appear in this publication for the first time. All rights reserved. In permission matters, contact Wadsworth Publishing Company, Inc., Belmont, California.

L. C. Cat. Card No.: 67–25147
Printed in the United States of America

preface

To be successful, an introductory study of any subject must somehow be both accurate and simple. The complexity of the subject should not be disguised, or the student will assume that the encyclopedia will serve him just as well as a ten- or fifteen-week course. But neither should the student be intimidated by networks of terminology that attempt to catalogue all the features of the subject to which he is now being exposed for the first time. Poetry is perhaps as difficult a subject as any he is likely to encounter. Because no two poems are alike, the elements of poetry cannot be classified. Descriptive terminology can take the student only so far, and then he is on his own. And yet many introductory books on poetry tempt the student to rely very heavily on the descriptive machinery of the introduction itself. The more detailed a book becomes, the less it will encourage the student to read poems as the irreducible units that they are.

This book is a fairly close reading of about fifteen short poems.

In planning the content of the chapters, I have assumed that the student will from the first be endeavoring to paraphrase each poem that he reads. To do this much he needs only a dictionary, a few hints from his instructor, and a big push. But developing a sensitivity to the style of a poem will require patience, both of the instructor and the student, and a minimal analytic vocabulary. To help the student assimilate such a vocabulary and subsequently put it to work when he reads other poems, I have divided the subject of style into what seem to me its most basic parts. Chapters 2, 3, and 4 are devoted, respectively, to the references, the relationships, and the sounds that are the poem. Before we can know what each of these contributes, we must know what it is; several kinds of diction, organization, and meter and rhythm are therefore described and illustrated separately.

With a few exceptions, I have tried to select poems (1) that are carefully controlled and (2) that illustrate the particular stylistic element in question. For the most part, I have also chosen poems that are rarely anthologized in the hope either that the instructor will devote class time to poems more frequently published or that the student himself will want to go to the anthologies, select those poems he finds most worthy of his attention, and apply what he may have learned from reading this book. The book is not meant to be used for more than a week in any given course. It is designed only to provide a brief but accurate vocabulary for discussing the style of the short poem, a vocabularly that the students might share without wasting class time, which can be more profitably spent in discussing individual poems. The value of the book, or of any introductory book on poetry, must ultimately depend on the extent to which it coerces the student to confide in his own discoveries about what goes on in the best poetry.

I wish to thank the following for their interest and help: John F. Adams, Carol Agee, Pete E. Clecak, Jerene Cline, Dennis G. Donavan, Diane Ewing, Harvey Gross, Daniel T. Havens, V. A. Kolve, and Compton Rees.

contents

1   *tone* 1
2   *diction* 9
3   *organization* 27
4   *meter and rhythm* 49
5   *two sonnets* 73

The style of the short poem

1

tone

When a poet writes a poem, he isn't talking *to* you, but rather to *you.*

Had I been able to deliver the previous sentence in person, you would have known the distinction I wanted you to understand by the tone of my voice. Because you are reading the sentence—not hearing it—and because the words in the phrase "talking to you" are the same in each instance, I have had to use italics so that you will begin to understand what I mean. The poet who knows his business uses far more refined stylistic techniques than either italics or a simple shift in the inflection of the voice. But he uses these techniques for precisely the same reason that I employ the cruder ones: We both want you to know more from our words than you could know if you were insensitive to the way we use these words. The purpose of this book is to illustrate a few of the stylistic techniques that you will find in lyric poetry and to provide you with a vocabulary for talking about them. There is no guarantee that reading the book will make you immediately sensitive to every poem that you read. But it won't hurt.

Now what does it mean to say that the poet talks to *you?* It means that when you read his poem he wants you to apply what you know or can imagine about a subject in order to achieve a detailed understanding of what that same subject was for him.

This Is Just to Say

I have eaten
the plums
that were in
the icebox

and which   5
you were probably
saving
for breakfast

Forgive me
they were delicious   10
so sweet
and so cold

If you read this poem carefully, you are likely to imagine yourself as either the forgiver or the forgiven, depending on your sex. From your own experience you know the sensation on your palate of cold, sweet fruit; and you can at least imagine this sensation's being so infectious that you might not be able to stop after eating one piece, or two, or five. You know, too, that forgiveness is not restricted only to the most severe interpersonal sins, but that it can and does extend to even the simplest domestic courtesies, like putting one's smelly socks in the clothes hamper or waiting until breakfast to eat some very inviting plums. In short, you can imagine what it would be like to live in the same house with the forgiver or the forgiven and feel that, if you wrote or read a note such as this, you would either be forgiven or forgive.

Or would you? What if you are or imagine being a spinster? A cook at a boarding house? What if you hate plums? Would this kind of forgiveness then have any relevance for you? If the answer is "no," the poem hasn't spoken to *you*. You will have read it and could say, accurately enough, that it spoke *to* you. But your inability to understand the very particular nature of the experience which the poem describes would mean that you and the poet were not, in the truest sense of the word, communicating.

In this particular instance I would have to judge that you, not the poet, were responsible for this lack of communication. His poem is basically very simple and clear. It is unpretentious in the sense that he clearly isn't asking you to consider the experience he describes as a real contender in importance to Macbeth's murdering the king; but it is carefully controlled and therefore succeeds very well at what it does try. Some poems attempting no more than this one are not controlled, in that they make it very difficult for you to understand the poet's experience even when you suspend those private pre-dispositions of your own that might intrude between your understanding of the poem and the poem itself. Think again of the poem you read a few minutes ago. Imagine that you really do hate plums, that they make you break out in a rash. Now if you aren't able to forget, while you engage the poem, that most people aren't affected by plums in this way, you won't understand the poem. And if you should in turn write an intensely serious poem cursing plums because of what they do to you, you will have to be ready to be misunderstood. The tone of your poem—what it is supposed to say to *me* and to *everyone*—would be incomprehensible to all who do not share your peculiar allergy.

This example is ludicrous enough that you might be tempted to dismiss it as irrelevant. In fact, poems about plums have a way of seeming not to be poems at all. Even if it can be admitted that "This Is Just to Say" talks to *you*, what it tells you is so small that it seems merely anecdotal. Poetry, you might tell me, has bigger things to do. And I would agree with you. But poems about big subjects are no less obligated to communicate with you than poems about small ones, and both big and small poems meet this obligation in the same way. The difficulties that the poet faces are no different when he talks about plums than when he talks about death. With either subject he must record enough private, personal, particular information to convince you that he hasn't too greatly oversimplified his experience in relating it to you. At the same time, however, he must be able to make the very fine distinction between "enough" private information and "too much" of it. His poem should not be so public, impersonal, and general that it seems totally obvious—nor should it use language in so private a way that its meaning remains inaccessible.

To be sure, poetry is a private thing. A good poem—when you are at your best in reading it—tells you something so singular and so inimitable that you will not be able to tell someone else precisely what you have experienced in reading it. But in order for you to know that you have encountered the poem itself, and not simply your idea of the poem, the poem must also have a public element, an element that enables many people to respond to it in much the same way. Just because different people's responses will never be identical in every detail, the poet should not despair of communicating and thus proceed to be obscure. On the contrary, it is a very good reason for him to say what he has to say as clearly as he can.

Insofar as a poet is not clear, he will be talking not to you but to himself. The temptation to talk to oneself is very great, and it is as easy to give in to the temptation in writing a small poem as it is in writing a big one. It is more difficult to write a clear poem about a tiny subject than to write an unclear poem about a very big one. And it is harder still, of course, to write a clear poem about a big subject. Had you written your invective against plums, you would probably have realized that I might not take the poem seriously. You might have seen the humor yourself and revised the poem in such a way that I would know you were writing a mock invective, pointing fun at the ridiculousness of anger over such a trivial malady. The subject of your poem would be the same before and after revision: the rash that you get from eating plums. But the tone of the revised version would be very different; and that change of tone would probably increase the clarity of the poem. But what if your subject had not been plums, but rather love, or death? If you suspected that your original version of a poem about death wasn't clear, you would have far less latitude in altering the tone than you would in a poem about plums, for you would be much slower to concede your private responses to this subject. Nor would I be as ready to concede mine. If we are to communicate effectively about these more ambitious subjects, then, your task—and mine—will be considerably greater than it would have been with the simpler subject.

But I have been speaking too hypothetically. Let's look at two poems, both of them relatively clear and both, really, about the same subject—love and death and poetry. Notice, though, the difference in their tones. If you miss this difference, one or both of the poems will have failed to communicate with you.

How many paltry, foolish, painted things,
That now in coaches trouble every street,
Shall be forgotten, whom no poet sings,
Ere they be well wrapped in their winding-sheet?
Where I to thee eternity shall give,   5
When nothing else remaineth of these days,
And queens hereafter shall be glad to live
Upon the alms of thy superfluous praise.
Virgins and matrons, reading these my rimes,
Shall be so much delighted with thy story   10
That they shall grieve they lived not in these times,
To have seen thee, their sex's only glory:
    So shalt thou fly above the vulgar throng,
    Still to survive in my immortal song.

Like as the waves make towards the pebbled shore,
So do our minutes hasten to their end,
Each changing place with that which goes before,
In sequent toil all forwards do contend.
Nativity, once in the main of light,   5
Crawls to maturity, wherewith being crowned,
Crooked eclipses 'gainst his glory fight,
And Time that gave doth now his gift confound.
Time doth transfix the flourish set on youth
And delves the parallels in beauty's brow,   10
Feeds on the rarities of nature's truth,
And nothing stands but for his scythe to mow.
    And yet to times in hope my verse shall stand,
    Praising thy worth, despite his cruel hand.

In trying to define the resemblances and differences between these poems, we will begin with a simple and very brief paraphrase of each.

> *First poem:* How many women who are now alive will be forgotten, even before they are buried, because no poet has celebrated them in his verse? When everything that now lives is gone, my verse will still make you eternal; and queens living after us will be content to receive whatever leftover praise they might charitably be given. After reading my poems, other women will grieve that they could not have lived now, so that they might have seen you—the one of their sex whose qualities so exceed those of all others that you are truly your "sex's only glory." In this way you will ascend above those who need not be immortalized, and in my poetry you will survive.

> *Second poem:* Time moves in the same way that waves proceed toward the shore. The newborn child moves very slowly into the prime of life; as soon as he has reached it, he begins to decline, for Time works to destroy the mature human being that it has developed. Time pierces what we find attractive in the young, digs into the features that make one beautiful, feeds on those who were by nature the most uniquely blessed; nothing rises but to be cut down by Time. And yet despite Time's cruelties, my poetry, which praises your value, will survive.

The purpose of this book is to introduce you to the fundamental stylistic techniques that you will encounter in the poems you read, and the paraphrases that I have just given tell you very little, really, about the style of their respective poems. But unless we begin with a simple and accurate explication of a poem, we will not know what the style of that poem is doing. If the poet is in control of what he tells you, if his poem is clear, the paraphrasable part of the poem will be in such close conjunction with everything else that is going on in it that you will have a great deal of difficulty distinguishing between the two. A good poem is never just a paraphrasable subject that the poet has more or less fortuitously "styled." Nor are the paraphrases above limited strictly to the nonstylistic aspects of the poems.

It is important to consider not only what the words of a poem mean but *the way* they mean; for it is only by virtue of their own very individual styles that separate poems tell you something that you will find nowhere else in the world. In the two poems above, if we didn't attempt to pursue this distinction between what the words mean and the way they mean, our concerns with them as separate statements about human experience would dovetail into a single and very general response to both. What the words of both poems mean, in the most general sense, is that, although death is busy leveling everything else, the poet earns immortality for his lady. It is when we begin to consider the way the words mean that we see what very different priorities each poet has assigned to the subjects of love, death, and poetry. Once we notice the most general stylistic features of the poems, we can see that the first poet shows much more interest in the lady than the second does. The first poet tells his lady that his praise for her will earn her immortality. The second poet, although he tells his lady essentially the same thing, tells it almost as an afterthought to his twelve-line disquisition on the insidiousness of death.

To say this much about the tonal differences between the poems, however, is only to begin. There can be no simple formula by which to decide what your response to a given poem should be, for formulae have a way of forcing you to ignore the most individual characteristics of your subject—the characteristics that you must learn not to ignore if you are to discover what the style of a poem tells you. The tone of each poem you read will differ absolutely from that of the next, whereas the general subject matter of two of them might, as in the case of our sonnets, suggest close similarities. This book should encourage you to ask these questions about how the words of any given poem are working. (1) What is the nature of the poem's diction: To what do the words of the poem refer? (2) How is the poem organized: In what way do the words of the poem relate to one another? (3) How do the meter and rhythm of the poem contribute to the tone of the poem: What is the relevance of the way the poem sounds? We will concern ourselves with these questions in the next three chapters and then return, in the final chapter, to take a closer look at the tone of the two poems on love, death, and poetry.

2

diction

When you read any poem, your first impulse should be to want to know why the poet has used these words and not some others. One of the poet's first concerns in choosing the words of his poem is to refer you to those things that he wants you to imagine as you read it. In this chapter I will talk about the kinds of references that words can have within the context of the poem, and I will try to prompt you to consider two things that you might overlook if you were concerned only with paraphrasing the poem: (1) The way a poet uses a word can cause it to refer to something *other* than what it refers to outside his poem. (2) The way a poet uses a word can cause it to refer to *more* things than it refers to outside his poem. The good poet says precisely what he means. But in doing so he counts heavily on your paying close attention to the words of his poem and the kinds of things that they represent.

Out of context, the words of our language refer to one of three categories of things. First, there are the strictly grammatical agents, such as "and," "the," "however," and "to." The words in this group refer to neither activity nor object but are essential, nevertheless, to the sense of what we say. A second group of words, like "thinking," "peace," "contagious," and "solution," have *abstract* referents; their referents cannot be experienced by the senses as readily as can those of words like "running," "cat," "black," and "Fluff." These words belong to a third group, which we label *concrete*. When you are dealing with words of the second and third groups, remember that it is not the words themselves that are either abstract or concrete, but rather the activities and objects to which these words refer. All words are abstractions of our experience. The word "cat" is just as abstract as the word "peace." If you forget this very basic fact, you will be tempted to pay too little attention to the context in which a word appears, and you might therefore replace the context the author has carefully supplied with your own.

When, in a poem, you encounter a word that refers to a concrete activity or object, the poet may very well want you to think about all the characteristics that the activity or object has had in your own private experience. But because he has attempted to supply you with a context by which you can know what that activity or object was for him in the particular experience his poem describes, you are not at liberty to treat a concrete word as a real thing. The cat that a poet talks about may indeed have been a real cat, but it was the real cat as he experienced it. It is his obligation to provide you with as much information about the cat as he considers relevant and communicable; it is yours to try to comprehend the cat's relevance to the poet. Both of these obligations—the poet's and your own—take place within the context of the poem; and until they are met, the tone of the poem remains inaccessible.

But it is no less important for you to pay close attention to the context of a poem when its referents are abstract. There are poems that refer almost exclusively to abstract activities and objects. Here is one of the best.

> In whose will is our peace? Thou happiness,
> Thou ghostly promise, to thee I confess
> Neither in thine nor love's nor in that form
> Disquiet hints at have I yet been warm;

And if I rest not till I rest in thee   5
Cold as thy grace, whose hand shall comfort me?

The poet has defined a complicated and intensely personal phenomenon in very few words. Because the phenomenon, despair, is internal
rather than external, the poet has chosen a diction that refers to
abstract rather than to concrete categories. This decision was a
stylistic one. He could have chosen, presumably, to define his despair through some kind of vivid externalization of the emotion
(although speculating about what a poet might have done can become foolish); but it is unlikely that he could have controlled such a
definition with the precision he demonstrates here.

Our understanding of the poem depends upon our locating the
abstract referents of the words "happiness," "ghostly promise,"
"love," and "that form/ Disquiet hints at." Their nature becomes
clear only when we recognize the direction of the two questions
that the poet asks. The questions are in effect the same; in both, the
poet asks where he might find peace. The answers to the questions,
however, differ in one very important way. The question "In whose
will is our peace?" contains a trace of optimism, for it suggests at
least the possibility that there may be some divine being, some
person who wills that we be at peace. The poet proceeds to consider
possible answers to his original question. The first alternative is
"happiness," which the poet addresses both as itself and as "ghostly
promise." Notice that "happiness," as well as its appositive, "ghostly
promise," is addressed almost personally. The pronouns "Thou,"
"thee," and "thine" subtly echo the whisper of optimism in the first
question, since they suggest that "happiness"—like whoever wills our
peace—might have a personal identity. But the second and third
alternatives, "love" and "that form/ Disquiet hints at," are not
addressed directly. And we begin to have a sense, which is deepened
by the negative quality of the "neither/nor" formula, that the poet
has not been able to answer his question. He can only pose another
question, almost identical to the first. Whereas an attempt to answer
the first question involves a serious examination of certain alternatives, any real attempt to answer the second must be undertaken
with a recognition that the best possible answers have been considered and rejected.

And yet what are these alternatives, and why are we to believe that they are in fact the best possible answers? The first alternative is the composite reference of "happiness" and "ghostly promise." When you first encounter the word "happiness," you must take it in its broadest possible sense: the happiness, whatever its source or manifestation, that would have provided the poet with the peace he has not found. But the referent of "happiness" becomes much more particular when we consider the word in conjunction with its appositive. "Ghostly promise" refers us to the kind of otherworldly consolation that satisfies those who have a strong faith in an afterlife. The adjective "ghostly" explicitly signifies, or denotes, immateriality, spirituality, that which is incorporeal but nonetheless real. But notice the tone of this word. It can implicitly suggest, or connote, a great many things; and one cannot define all that it connotes. Within the carefully controlled context of the poem, however, it should be clear which connotations the poet wants us to feel are the most relevant to the particular experience he describes. The promise is "ghostly," rather than "spiritual" (or some other denotative equivalent), because the poet wants us to know very particularly (1) that, despite his wishes to the contrary, the promise of an afterlife is no more real to him than a ghost story; and (2) that thinking about his mortality causes him a kind of terror. By placing "happiness" and "ghostly promise" in apposition, the poet makes the former become very particular indeed. "Happiness," for him, is predicated upon the credibility of an afterlife.

"Love" is the second alternative in his search for peace. Like "happiness," "love" must first be taken in its broadest sense; but unlike "happiness," it is not followed by a qualifying term, and so there is no subsequent narrowing of the referent. I think we can say that the referent of "love" in this poem is interpersonal love in any form.

The final alternative is "that form/ Disquiet hints at," and the referents here are also difficult to locate. Let us review quickly what we have been told about the poet's attempts to find peace. Because he cannot believe that otherworldly consolation will come to him after he leaves this life, the "ghostly promise" of "happiness" has offered him no peace. Nor has he found in life a love that compensates for his anxiety about death. The scope of the alternatives of "happiness" and "love" suggests, in however quiet and understated a way, that in his life he has found nothing to affirm. His "disquiet" at having failed in such a search "hints at" another "form" than life: It hints at death. Since he has not been able to affirm his life, perhaps he should affirm the leaving of it; perhaps he should, to quote another poet, "praise the annihilation of the pit" and feel that death itself will bring him a kind of peace. But like the other alternatives, the third has offered him no warmth.

Precisely because they are so comprehensive, these three alternatives are the best answer to his original question. The poet, remember, has asked a rather big question, and he has found no answer. He wants us to come away from his poem with some accurate sense of his despair. And unless we are convinced that he has considered the most viable kinds of affirmation and found them insufficient, we will be tempted to tell him to go back and take a closer look at his experience. Of course, we might tell him this even if we are convinced that he has overlooked little that might have provided him with hope; but we would do so with more respect for his unmistakable anxiety.

The most notable stylistic feature of this poem is that its diction refers us almost exclusively to abstract categories. Even those few words which, out of this immediate context, refer to sensible qualities come close to having abstract referents. In using the words "warm" and "cold," the poet is more concerned with the contrast between the two as they relate to his search than with the physical characteristics of warmth and coldness. In one of his other poems he speaks of the "child's game where you grow warm and warmer." He is playing no child's game here, to be sure, but something of the same notion is still operating. I don't mean to imply that the words "warm" and "cold" are not intended to connote all the things that we are likely to associate with the very real qualities of warmth and coldness. Indeed, if we do not permit the sudden contrast between "cold" and "thy grace" to register in us with some suggestion of what coldness really is, we will miss one of the most important tonal elements in the poem. But like the poet's use of the word "hand"—which decidedly refers to no real hand, since the answer to the question "whose hand?" must finally be "no one's"—the words "warm" and "cold" take referents that are more abstract than those they would take out of context.

Although the diction of the following poem is as antithetical to that of "In whose will" as any diction you are likely to find, the poem will be similarly inaccessible to you if you are not aware of the poem's style.

Blueflags

I stopped the car
to let the children down
where the streets end
in the sun
at the marsh edge   5
and the reeds begin
and there are small houses
facing the reeds
and the blue mist
in the distance   10
with grapevine trellises
with grape clusters
small as strawberries
on the vines
and ditches   15
running springwater
that continue the gutters
with willows over them.
The reeds begin
like water at a shore   20
their pointed petals waving
dark green and light.
But blueflags are blossoming
in the reeds
which the children pluck   25
chattering in the reeds
high over their heads
which they part
with bare arms to appear
with fists of flowers   30
till in the air
there comes the smell
of calamus
from wet, gummy stalks.

If you decide that the style of the poem is inviting you to imagine that the words "reeds," "mist," "grapevine trellises," "vines," "springwater," "blueflags," and "calamus" refer to symbols or some other abstract category, or if you think that these words refer to anything other than the concrete objects they describe, you will not know what the poem is about. It is about real reeds, real mist, real grapevine trellises. It is about these things as they are experienced within a short period of time by the speaker of the poem.

Contrast the diction of "In whose will" with that of "Blueflags." In the former poem the diction evokes no specific sensory experience; warmth, coldness, and that nonexistent hand of comfort are referred to in such a way that we pay only indistinct attention to them as physical realities. The diction of "Blueflags," on the other hand, takes us through four of the five senses and asks that we reconstruct at least forty distinct sensory impressions that the speaker of the poem experienced. In line 4 we have a tactile and visual impression of the sun. A great many visual details follow, through line 25. The "chattering" children introduce us to aural sensory impression; the "smell of calamus" refers to the olfactory sense; and the poem concludes with another tactile impression, "wet, gummy stalks."

The diction of the poem thus invites us to imagine employing most of our senses and refers us directly to concrete activities and objects that our senses should engage. But the diction is also doing considerably more. The poem uses a relatively high proportion of words that refer us neither to abstract nor to concrete entities. These words are the grammatical agents: articles, conjunctions, prepositions, and relative pronouns. Look at the first sentence of the poem again, noticing the way that these grammatical agents are used.

> I stopped *the* car
> *to* let *the* children down
> *where the* streets end
> *in the* sun
> *at the* marsh edge
> *and the* reeds begin
> *and there* are small houses
> facing *the* reeds
> *and the* blue mist

> *in the* distance
> *with* grapevine trellises
> *with* grape clusters
> small *as* strawberries
> *on the* vines
> *and* ditches
> running springwater
> *that* continue *the* gutters
> *with* willows *over* them.

All but four of the eighteen lines begin with a word that has neither an abstract nor a concrete referent. This syntactical pattern, or word order, is most noticeable in lines 3 through 7, which begin, respectively, "where the," "in the," "at the," "and the," "and there." The same kind of repetition extends throughout the sentence and the poem, and it imparts a tone of unmistakable simplicity.

Because its diction and syntax are so repetitive that they drone, is the sentence a bad one? If the sentence were taken out of context, the answer would have to be "yes." But given the subject of this poem, the style of the sentence is very appropriate. What is it about his subject, then, that makes the poet want to suggest that he is a maker of primitive sentences? The experience that he is describing is a very small one. We can tell that much by recognizing that the nouns, verbs, adjectives, and adverbs refer us to a very specific landscape and ask us to respond to this landscape in an uncomplicated way. The tone of the poem is certainly not one of indifference to the landscape; but neither does the landscape come to represent any complex intellectual or emotional states. Unlike "In whose will," this poem is concerned almost wholly with external experience. It is therefore important to the poet that he preserve as much of this external detail as the language will permit. We receive the details in precisely the order that they presented themselves to his consciousness. His impressions succeeded one another so rapidly that he has chosen to deny them the kinds of relationships they might have with one another in a more studied sentence; he seems to feel that if he presented his impressions in a tightly constructed declarative sentence, avoiding the clumsiness of repeated words and syntactical patterns, he would deprive each separate impression of some of its integrity.

The abruptness of several of the transitions also tends to emphasize the separateness of each detail and the discrete sensory impression it created in the poet. For example, notice that the description in lines 5–17 is so casually organized that the spatial relationships in the scene are not immediately clear.

> and there are small houses
> facing the reeds
> and the blue mist
> in the distance
> with grapevine trellises
> with grape clusters
> small as strawberries
> on the vines
> and ditches
> running springwater
> that continue the gutters
> with willows over them.

Are the "grapevine trellises" on the lots of the "small houses"? Are these houses "facing the reeds/ and the blue mist/. . . and ditches/ running springwater"? Where, precisely, are the "willows"? Are they over the "ditches" or over the "gutters"? The answers to these questions are not as important as the fact that a stylistic device has caused us to ask them, for the diction of the poem, as well as the way it is used, tells us that the poet is far more concerned with the separate items themselves than he is with the relationships between these items.

Unlike "In whose will," "Blueflags" does not talk about a lifetime's experience; it talks instead about a once-in-a-lifetime experience. Because the experience itself was unique, the poet wants the tone of the poem to reflect his excitement, and so his diction approximates the rapidity of his sensory impressions. But for all its excitement, the experience he describes does not have the import of a subject such as despair. Accordingly, his diction refers us to the sensory impressions quietly, accurately; and there is no suggestion that the details in the scene have evoked any very complicated internal response in the poet.

The diction of this next poem differs noticeably from that in either of the poems we have discussed previously in this chapter; but like each of them, the poem is carefully controlled, and its style and subject complement one another effectively.

> The earth with thunder torn, with fire blasted,
> With waters drowned, with windy palsy shaken
> Cannot for this with heaven be distasted,
> Since thunder, rain, and winds from earth are taken.
> Man torn with love, with inward furies blasted,   5
> Drowned with despair, with fleshly lustings shaken,
> Cannot for this with heaven be distasted:
> Love, fury, lustings out of man are taken.
> Then, man, endure thyself; those clouds will vanish,
> Life is a top which whipping sorrow driveth;   10
> Wisdom must bear what our flesh cannot banish;
> The humble lead, the stubborn bootless striveth.
>   Or man, forsake thyself, to heaven turn thee;
>   Her flames enlighten nature, never burn thee.   6

Whereas the diction of "In whose will" referred us almost exclusively to abstract conditions, and that of "Blueflags" referred us to concrete ones, the diction of this poem refers more equally than either of the others to both the abstract and the concrete. The balance between abstract and concrete is so equal, in fact, that we might almost imagine the poet keeping a close, quantitative watch on the nature of his referents. There are ten nouns with concrete referents: "earth," "thunder," "fire," "waters," "palsy," "rain," "clouds," "top," "flesh," "flames." There are another ten with abstract referents: "love," "furies," "despair," "lustings," "life," "sorrow," "wisdom," "humble," "stubborn," "nature." Of the verbs, adjectives, and adverbs, there are ten with concrete referents: "torn," "blasted," "drowned," "windy," "shaken," "fleshly," "whipping," "driveth," "turn," "burn." And there are ten with abstract ones: "distasted," "taken," "inward," "endure," "vanish," "bear," "banish," "lead," "striveth," "forsake." With the exception of those words that we would classify as grammatical agents, this count has overlooked only three words: "bootless," "heaven," and "enlighten."

"The earth with thunder torn" differs from the two preceding poems in the function of its diction as well as in the proportions of abstract and of concrete referents. The poet of "In whose will" is concerned with the ways in which his experience has affected him internally; he is almost entirely unconcerned with external physical phenomena. The poet of "Blueflags" is just as unconcerned with internal conditions. He reports the presence of the marsh edge, grapevine trellises, blueflags, and calamus; but he does not write of how they affected him internally. In each of these poems, then, the poet devotes his attention almost exclusively to either internal or external phenomena. But the poet of "The earth with thunder torn," as we can see from the balance between the abstract and the concrete, seems to be concerned with both.

A poet, or for that matter anyone who uses language, has the prerogative of synthesizing his internal and external experiences so that neither is treated in isolation from the other; such synthesis is accomplished through some form of analogy. The function of analogy is to suggest that two or more items with something in common probably have considerably more in common. "Life is a top which whipping sorrow driveth." It is unlikely that you would say a life of sorrow is identical to a whirling top. The two are in fact very separate affairs; and not the least of their differences is that the first is internal and essentially abstract, and the second is external and concrete. But once the words have introduced you to a similarity between the two, your sense of the very real separation between them is at least temporarily blunted. You are not, however, asked to suspend the associations you might normally make with either a life of sorrow or a top. The characteristics peculiar to each half of the analogy are retained. But your response to the analogy will be very different from your response to a diction referring you exclusively to one half or to the other; for the analogy causes you to focus on that aspect of sorrow that the poet is most interested in communicating. Thus, the analogy is simply another of the methods by which the poet can control your intellectual and emotional response to his subject.

The analogies that operate in "The earth with thunder torn" are as explicit as any you are likely to find.

> The earth with thunder torn, with fire blasted,
> With waters drowned, with windy palsy shaken
> Cannot for this with heaven be distasted,
> Since thunder, rain, and winds from earth are taken.

The first four lines refer us to the violence done to the earth by the natural forces of thunder, fire, water, and wind, and state that the earth has no cause to blame heaven for this violence, since these forces are products of the earth. Notice how closely the form of these four lines is imitated in the second four.

> Man torn with love, with inward furies blasted,
> Drowned with despair, with fleshly lustings shaken,
> Cannot for this with heaven be distasted:
> Love, fury, lustings out of man are taken.

The repetition of this form lends even greater credence to the two analogies: the first between the external, concrete forces of nature and the internal, abstract forces in man, and the second between the earth and man in respect to their lack of justification in blaming heaven for their very similar plights. The analogy works in such a way that the second time the words "torn," "blasted," "drowned," and "shaken" are used, they retain the concrete referents that they had the first time but are qualified by being coupled with nouns that take abstract referents.

Although it receives its most detailed development in the first eight lines, the analogy between external and internal conditions does not end with line 8. Lines 9 through 12 define the first of two alternatives that man has in responding to his plight.

> Then, man, endure thyself; those clouds will vanish,
> Life is a top which whipping sorrow driveth;
> Wisdom must bear what our flesh cannot banish;
> The humble lead, the stubborn bootless striveth.

Man may resign himself stoically to his situation, knowing that, since the things of this world and flesh produce only sorrow, the wisest course is to bear with humility what cannot be banished with stubbornness. The two concluding lines offer the second alternative:

> Or man, forsake thyself, to heaven turn thee;
> Her flames enlighten nature, never burn thee.

The preceding twelve lines have dealt with worldly concerns; the only reference to heaven has emphasized its innocence in regard to the external and internal torments that man undergoes on this earth. Now, for the first time, we are given a definition of heaven's interaction with man and his world. It is here that we must consider the referents of the words "heaven" and "enlighten." The first word, presumably, is abstract; but notice that the poet has characterized heaven as exhibiting concrete manifestations: flames. What do these flames do? Unlike those of the earth, which burn, the flames of heaven "enlighten" the natural world. To "enlighten" is literally to "make light"—a concrete phenomenon. As it is generally used, however, the word means "clarify," which is decidedly abstract.

The analogy between the external and the internal is thus sustained throughout the poem. By calling attention to the difference in effect between the flames of heaven and the flames of earth, the poet stresses the contrast between heaven and earth; but he also recognizes that the success of his definitions of both heaven and earth depends upon the credibility with which his poem synthesizes external and internal experiences. Man's relationship to heaven is an internal and abstract one, to be sure. A belief in heaven requires an intellectual and emotional response that might be completely unsupported by external, concrete evidence of the existence of such a place. But since man's experience this side of heaven is a composite of abstract and concrete, internal and external, the reality of heaven can be made more immediate if it is characterized in a similarly composite way. It is the diction of the poem, as it operates analogically, that makes this composite possible.

If you stop for a moment to consider the kinds of diction that you have seen operating in the poems we have discussed in this chapter, you will remember that the diction of "In whose will" referred hardly at all to sensory details, and the diction of "Blue-flags" referred to no intellectual concepts. Since our experience is a combination of sensory and intellectual activity, "The earth with thunder torn" might seem to you a more complete representation of what it is to be a human being than either of the first two. You might be able to defend such a judgment, but to do so you would have to take into account the fact that the poet is in every case free to choose the proportion of abstract and concrete references that he believes most appropriate to the subject he wishes to define. His poem should be judged unfavorably only if he does not make clear to you the reasons for his choice of diction. The three poems that we have examined are very successful in showing why their respective poets made the choices that they did.

In discussing "The earth with thunder torn," I mentioned that the analogy between the external and internal conditions which the poem defined was developed in an explicit manner. By contrast, here is a poem in which the analogies are implicitly developed.

Old Woman

Not even in darkest August,
When the mysterious insects
Marry loudly in the black weeds,
And the woodbine, limp after rain,
In the cooled night is more fragrant,   5
Do you gather in any slight
Harvest to yourself. Deep whispers
Of slight thunder, horizons off,
May break your thin sleep, but awake
You cannot hear them. Harsh gleaner   10
Of children, grandchildren—remnants
Of nights now forever future—
Your dry, invisible shudder
Dies on this porch, where, uninflamed,
You dread the oncoming seasons,   15
Repose in the electric night.

This poem is a difficult one. In the first sentence, the main verb is delayed until the sixth line. The sentence addresses the old woman, though somewhat indirectly, and tells her that she is able to harvest nothing—even "in darkest August," when the atmosphere and landscape are the most lush and productive. To speak of her as a harvester is of course to speak analogically, and if we are to understand more particularly why she is a harvester, even a harvester of nothing, we must read further. As she dozes, the distant thunder registers with her enough to wake her; but once she is awake, she cannot hear it. She is old, as the title tells us, and exercises so little control over her body that it responds to stimuli of which she herself is not conscious. The third sentence again picks up the harvester motif. What she has "gleaned" are offspring, who are "remnants/ Of nights now forever future." Her children and grand-children are all that remain for her to glean. But they are gleaned only in the sense that they will in turn procreate and thus engender her seed in future generations. She has outlived her own reproductive capacities, and whatever she harvests from the seed she originally planted in her children will be harvested in those nights for her "now forever future," in which her progeny will copulate and conceive. In distinct contrast to those nights to come is her night, this night, on "this porch." Here she reposes, "uninflamed" by either the fecundity of the landscape or the sexual impulses that are rife in the "mysterious insects" as well as in her own children and grand-children, and fears the colder seasons that will soon come.

The diction tells us some very particular things about this old woman's internal condition and external surroundings as she reposes here on "this porch." The relationship between internal and external, though, is very different from the relationship between the words "life" and "top" in the line "Life is a top which whipping sorrow driveth." The metaphor that joins the abstract reference "life" and the concrete reference "top" is perfectly explicit: "Life is a top." The more extended metaphor between the external and internal tearing, blasting, drowning, and shaking is also explicit. The diction of "Old Woman" is no less analogical than that of "The earth with thunder torn"; however, the relationship between the literal, external, and concrete references and the figurative, internal, and abstract ones is stated in "The earth with thunder torn" and suggested in "Old Woman."

In the first sentence of "Old Woman," there is a distinct though unstated analogy between literal and figurative harvesting. Were she a literal harvester, the diction that refers us to her surroundings—"darkest August," "mysterious insects," "woodbine," "rain"—would serve a literal function only. Were she literally a harvester, we could expect her to be grateful for the summer rain, and we could imagine that her relationship to all the details of her surroundings would not extend beyond working in the fields under a dark sky to the sounds of the insects. It is in fact important to the analogy that we do imagine her as a literal harvester. The energy and skill that the poet has devoted to the words that take concrete referents should convince us that the evocation of a very real August landscape is important to his definition of the old woman. But in order to understand the precise function of these details of the landscape we must look at them within the context of the complete poem.

It is not until the third sentence that we learn why the old woman is not a harvester in a strictly literal sense. She is a gleaner not of inanimate crops but of children and grandchildren, and her gleaning is at an end, except in regard to those "nights now forever future," through which she will be preserved in the children and children's children of her grandchildren. The implications of her sterility are the more precisely defined because the diction refers us to her literal, external, and concrete surroundings. The analogy contrasts her sterility—the internal condition that the poet defines—with the fertility that surrounds her. And the nature of that analogy is implicit, rather than explicit, in the diction of the poem.

There are related and still more subtle analogies operating within the poem. In contrast to

> darkest August,
> When the mysterious insects
> Marry loudly in the black weeds,
> And the woodbine, limp after rain,
> In the cooled night is more fragrant,

and to "Deep whispers/ Of slight thunder, horizons off," the old woman's "dry, invisible shudder/ Dies on this porch, where, unin-flamed," she dreads "the oncoming seasons," reposes.

The diction refers us to characteristics that particularize even further her external and internal context: the dampness of the surrounding landscape as it contrasts with the dryness of the woman herself. Her productivity, in contrast with that of the fornicating insects, is reduced to an "invisible shudder," not in the lush and cool blackness of the fragrant woodbine but rather on "this porch." Her sterility, her dryness, is thus a concrete phenomenon. But the dry-ness also implies a more abstract contrast with the activity in the landscape. She is not an insect. Unlike them, she is capable of harshness, capable—perhaps most importantly—of dreading "the on-coming seasons." As a human being she has the capacity to abstract herself from concrete phenomena. Unlike the agents of fertility in the landscape, she is aware, in however limited a way, of her own plight. Her awareness may indeed exclude both a sensitivity to the lush details that surround her and the corresponding apprehension of how drastically she contrasts with the active richness of those details. It is by means of this contrast that we are able to understand the indifference of time and, accordingly, the simple finality of death. But if by senile innocence she is spared the pain of knowing her fate distinctly, we are not spared; we recognize that time and death will work no differently on us than they have worked and will work on her. The external world, with its thunder "horizons off," will persist when we and our internal harvestings, dryness, and fears have gone.

It is the burden of the poem's diction to locate the old woman in a precisely realized literal setting and to suggest for that setting the figurative implications of fertility, timelessness, and perpetual life. Let us once again contrast this poem's diction with that of "The earth with thunder torn." Both poems, as we have said, make use of analogies. A top is not life; a landscape is not fertility, timelessness, and perpetual existence. When we encounter either analogy, we must recognize that words that out of context take only concrete referents (a top is a top; a landscape is a landscape) have acquired abstract referents within the context of the poem (a top is both a top and life; the landscape is both the landscape and fertility). But the way in which the literal levels of each poem are controlled, so that we might know the figurative meaning of the details, differs noticeably. The associations that we have had with tops would rarely lead us to think them analogous to life, and so the poet links top and life by a strictly grammatical means: "Life *is* a top." Our associations with the concrete objects and activities to which the diction in "Old Woman" refers us will very definitely lead us to think these objects and activities not only analogous to fertility but perhaps even identical with it. That these concrete objects and fertility are not identical the poet knows; for concrete objects are nothing more than concrete objects and cannot mean. But the poet has been careful to describe these objects in such a way that your response, if you are reading carefully, will clearly be affected by the figurative implications that are vital to his definition.

However necessary it may be as a preliminary step, paraphrase never exhausts the energy of words. A word in a poem will refer you to your own very private experiences, and many of these experiences will be irrelevant to that word as the poet has used it. With practice, you will more quickly be able to know which of your associations complement the poet's definition and which do not; when you are able to make this distinction with some confidence, the diction of the poem will be able to do its appropriate work.

3

organization

In the last chapter we focused on individual words—the smallest units of a poem—and tried to define what we can learn about a poet's subject by paying careful attention to his choice of words. We will now approach the poem from the opposite direction, looking first at the structures of complete poems and then gradually returning to a concern with the individual words that constitute these structures. Diction and organization, obviously, are not separable elements in a poem. The words themselves and the structure they form are a single, inextricable entity. In the preceding chapter, for example, although I tried to limit my examination of the poems to the element of diction, I inevitably talked about the relationships between individual words. A consideration of the kinds of relationships that exist between all parts of a poem is more specifically the province of this chapter. And while it is important to remember that each of the three stylistic elements—diction, organization, and meter and rhythm—is directly dependent upon the other two for its existence, you should attempt to sharpen your sensitivity to the nature of each element in order to appreciate more fully the kind of work that it does within the poem.

Any use of language necessarily involves a progression of thought; and it is the obligation of its author to convey to us why his statement proceeds as it does and how all of its parts relate to one another. Since there are perhaps as many ways of doing this as there are poems, we will discuss as many poems as possible, to avoid generalizing too hastily in our descriptions of the basic organizational techniques. So that a kind of control may operate throughout the comparison of the separate structures, all of the poems will deal generally with the same subject: death. We should try to answer these questions about the organization of each poem: (1) To what extent are the relationships between the parts of the poem explicit or implicit? (2) How do these relationships help in controlling our response to the subject of the poem?

The structure of the poem below is decidedly explicit.

In Time of Plague

Adieu, farewell earth's bliss,
This world uncertain is;
Fond are life's lustful joys,
Death proves them all but toys,
None from his darts can fly.   5
I am sick, I must die.
  Lord, have mercy on us!

Rich men, trust not in wealth,
Gold cannot buy you health;
Physic himself must fade,   10
All things to end are made,
The plague full swift goes by;
I am sick, I must die.
  Lord, have mercy on us!

Beauty is but a flower   15
Which wrinkles will devour:
Brightness falls from the air,
Queens have died young and fair,

Dust hath closed Helen's eye.
I am sick, I must die.   20
   Lord, have mercy on us!

Strength stoops unto the grave,
Worms feed on Hector brave,
Swords may not fight with Fate.
Earth still holds ope her gate.   25
Come! come! the bells do cry.
I am sick, I must die.
   Lord, have mercy on us!

Wit with his wantonness
Tasteth death's bitterness;   30
Hell's executioner
Hath no ears for to hear
What vain art can reply.
I am sick, I must die.
   Lord, have mercy on us!   35

Haste, therefore, each degree,
To welcome destiny.
Heaven is our heritage,
Earth but a player's stage;
Mount we unto the sky.   40
I am sick, I must die.
   Lord, have mercy on us!

Thomas Nashe

The poem presents the reflections of a man who finds himself
surrounded by the manifestations of death that accompany a plague.
The first stanza introduces us to the subject, and each of the middle
four declares—with a new series of examples in each stanza—that
everyone is mortal. The sixth stanza differs from the preceding ones
only in that its first sentence is in the imperative mood and that it
stands, because of the word "therefore," as a summation of the
foregoing examples.

    The principle that organizes these reflections is the refrain that
appears in the last two lines of each stanza:

      I am sick, I must die.
         Lord, have mercy on us!

This refrain defines very explicitly the relation of each stanza to the others. The reflections in each stanza have a common motive: The speaker of the poem is sick, intensely aware of his mortality, and imploring of God's mercy. The refrain is in fact so central to our understanding of the relationship of one stanza to another that, with the exception of the first and last stanzas, the order of the stanzas could be rearranged without consequence to the poem.

When we read this poem there can be no question about how the poem proceeds or how its parts relate. Despite the fact that the structure of the poem includes opening and closing stanzas that can pass as an introduction and a conclusion, what we learn from the poem does not involve an argumentative progression in any true sense of the term. Once we know that each stanza turns around the refrain, we know where we are at every point in the poem. We are with a man who is concerned about the imminence of death and the need for mercy to the exclusion of everything that does not illustrate the truth of these concerns to him. The refrain makes it perfectly explicit what gold, beauty, strength, and intelligence have in common within the context of his definition: None of them can save a man from death.

The transitions in the next poem are also explicit; but the progression from part to part is not nearly as static as the progression of "In Time of Plague."

Church Monuments

> While that my soul repairs to her devotion,
> Here I intomb my flesh, that it betimes
> May take acquaintance of this heap of dust;
> To which the blast of death's incessant motion,
> Fed with the exhalation of our crimes,   5
> Drives all at last. Therefore I gladly trust
>
> My body to this school, that it may learn
> To spell its elements, and find its birth
> Written in dusty heraldry and lines;
> Which dissolution sure doth best discern,   10
> Comparing dust with dust, and earth with earth.
> These laugh at jet, and marble put for signs,

To sever the good fellowship of dust,
And spoil the meeting. What shall point out them,
When they shall bow, and kneel, and fall down flat   15
To kiss those heaps, which now they have in trust?
Dear flesh, while I do pray, learn here thy stem
And true descent; that when thou shalt grow fat,

And wanton in thy cravings, thou mayst know,
That flesh is but the glass, which holds the dust   20
That measures all our time; which also shall
Be crumbled into dust. Mark, here below,
How tame those ashes are, how free from lust,
That thou mayst fit thyself against thy fall.

The poet is offering himself some highly complicated instructions, by constructing a formal argument that advances clause by clause. "While my soul is busy being devout," he begins, "I come before these gravestones, inside the church, in order for my body to acquaint itself with the dust that resides within each grave. Because we must die, we are all destined to become dust; and the force of death is made greater by our sins. For these reasons, I want my body to learn its nature and origin by looking at the names and dates that are inscribed upon the gravestones; dissolution, that process through which the corpse decays, must understand better than any the true nature of the body, for it is best able to discern the fine line that separates the dust of one body from that of another and that earth which is the product of a decayed body from that which is not. Dust and earth find it amusing that the gravestones should attempt to preserve the identity of the corpse. What will there be to commemorate these stones when they have themselves fallen and coupled with the dust whose identity they now presume to protect? Body, while I engage in prayer, I hope you will learn what you really are, so that when you are tempted to be gluttonous or undisciplined in your desires, you will know that you are merely an hourglass which measures the length of time your own dust will retain this form . . . until the hourglass itself crumbles. Look at these graves and notice how tame and free from lust is the dust of these corpses; do this in preparation for your own return to dust."

Unlike "In Time of Plague," the stanzas of this poem could hardly be rearranged. Although there is no refrain to tell us just what relationship each clause has to those that precede and follow it, the poet has not left such relationships to implication. Of the thirty-three clauses that are separated from one another by some form of punctuation, all but six begin with words that connect them to what has gone before. Notice the way in which most of the clauses in the first sixteen lines of the poem are introduced:

> *While that* my soul repairs to her devotion,
> *Here* I intomb my flesh, *that it* betimes
> May take acquaintance of this heap of dust;
> *To which* the blast of death's incessant motion,
> Fed with the exhalation of our crimes,
> Drives all at last. *Therefore* I gladly trust
>
> My body to this school, *that it* may learn
> To spell its elements, *and* find its birth
> Written in dusty heraldry and lines;
> *Which* dissolution sure doth best discern,
> Comparing dust with dust, *and* earth with earth.
> *These* laugh at jet, *and* marble put for signs,
>
> To sever the good fellowship of dust,
> *And* spoil the meeting. *What* shall point out them,
> *When* they shall bow, *and* kneel, *and* fall down flat
> To kiss those heaps, *which* now they have in trust?

We then have a shift in mood from declarative to imperative; and once the new sentence is under way we return again to the explicit connectives:

> Dear flesh, *while* I do pray, learn here thy stem
> And true descent; *that when* thou shalt grow fat,
>
> *And* wanton in thy cravings, thou mayst know,
> *That* flesh is but the glass, *which* holds the dust
> *That* measures all our time; *which* also shall
> Be crumbled into dust.

The final sentence is also imperative, and its clauses are also introduced conjunctively.

Mark, *here below,*
How tame those ashes are, *how* free from lust,
That thou mayst fit thyself against thy fall.

Just as the poet of "In Time of Plague" does not require that
you infer how gold, beauty, strength, and intelligence relate to one
another in his reflections on his own mortality but explains this
relationship in each stanza, so too are the relationships in "Church
Monuments" made explicit by the grammar of its sentences. The
important difference in organization between the two poems is that
"In Time of Plague" illustrates a fairly simple assertion, whereas
"Church Monuments" develops a complicated argument. The subjects of the poems resemble one another in a very general way: The
speakers are attempting to prepare themselves for death. But each
poem presents its own unique variation on this subject, and the
organizational procedures of each are appropriate to their respective
variations. The speaker of the first poem has been more or less
trapped in the midst of a plague; his death is imminent. He thus has
little leisure to formulate a complicated response to death—unlike
the one who comes before the church monuments quite of his own
choosing. But both poems are powerfully serious, the one that is
carefully developed no less so than the one that employs the insistent
refrain.

Like "In Time of Plague," the next poem has a refrain, but it
also has organizational elements that are implicit rather than explicit.

During Wind and Rain

They sing their dearest songs—
He, she, all of them—yea,
Treble and tenor and bass,
    And one to play;
With the candles mooning each face. . . .   5
    Ah, no; the years O!
How the sick leaves reel down in throngs!

They clear the creeping moss—
Elders and juniors—aye,
Making the pathways neat   10

And the garden gay;
And they build a shady seat. . . .
Ah, no; the years, the years;
See, the white storm-birds wing across!

They are blithely breakfasting all—   15
Men and maidens—yea,
Under the summer tree,
With a glimpse of the bay,
While pet fowl come to the knee. . . .
Ah, no; the years O!   20
And the rotten rose is ript from the wall.

They change to a high new house,
He, she, all of them—aye,
Clocks and carpets and chairs
On the lawn all day,   25
And brightest things that are theirs. . . .
Ah, no; the years, the years;
Down their carved names the rain-drop ploughs.

This time the refrain is in the sixth line of each stanza. The form of
the refrain varies slightly in the second and fourth stanzas from "Ah,
no; the years O!" to "Ah, no; the years, the years," but as an
organizing principle the refrain brings each stanza into an explicit
relationship with the others. What is common to the details presented in the first five lines of each stanza is their absolute vulnerabil-
ity to "the years, the years." After the rather light description of
the people and their activities in the first five lines of each stanza, it is
the refrain that prepares us for the unmistakably ominous suggestions
of the final line. The repetition of this pattern—five lines describing
the people, then the refrain, and then a descriptive line that causes us
to anticipate an unhappy ending—is a significant structural device; it
supplements the refrain by stressing the insistence and inevitability
of time's passing.

Our response to "In Time of Plague" is controlled by the
repetitive structure of the poem in the sense that we assimilate each
new piece of information into a more and more intense awareness of
the futility, for the speaker, of turning to the things of this world

for any kind of solace. Although the subject of "During Wind and Rain" is significantly different, something similar occurs as a result of its repetitive structure. Each of its stanzas is a variation on the last, and the effect of knowing that the people who are described will all eventually meet death is a cumulative one. The repetition of the second line in the final stanza suggests that the progression of the poem is at least faintly circular, and that "He, she, all of them" have been gathered quietly into this circle.

But are the stanzas of "During Wind and Rain" interchangeable, as were those of "In Time of Plague," or is there a second structural principle operating along with the refrain? Unlike "In Time of Plague," whose structure is rather static, the organization of this poem reflects very vividly the passage of time. The poet does not state the relationships between the steps in this temporal progression explicitly, but depends instead on our ability to make a few fairly basic associations. One of these associations concerns the four seasons. The sequence begins with winter, possibly during wind and rain, as "they" sing inside by candlelight. The second stanza— spring—describes them making their preparations for a summer in the garden, and in the third we find them "Under the summer tree." There are no explicit references to fall in the final stanza, but by this point the seasonal sequence has been suggested strongly enough that explicit references are not really necessary.

Since we move through the calendar as we read the poem, are we to assume that its structure refers us to a single cycle of the seasons? I don't think so. To be aware of the way in which the structure of the poem evokes a temporal progression, we must make another series of associations: The stanzas describe four distinct stages in the life of a single family, and each of these stages is separated by "the years." Stanza one presents the family when the children are quite young. The children provide the high notes, the mother the middle, the father the low. The second stanza suggests that the "juniors" have grown enough to help with the chores. In the third stanza they are older still: "Men and maidens"—some of them the children, and some the friends of the children—breakfast "blithely" "under the summer tree." With the final stanza the parents have anticipated the departure of their grown-up children, and the family is moving "to a high new house"—the house in which the parents, presumably, will die years later. The progression of the seasons is thus played against the progression of "the years," making us conscious of the relationships between each of the stanzas. And these relationships, without explicitly telling us so, imply the passing of the "brightest things" in the lives of each member of this family —or any family.

There is still a third implication in the temporal structure of the poem. Notice that the activities described in the first five lines of stanzas two, three, and four cannot possibly be occurring "during wind and rain." The title must refer, then, to the final lines of the stanzas, all of which might well take place during a storm. When we encounter the final line of the poem, "Down their carved names the rain-drop ploughs," we recognize that the present-tense verbs that have been used throughout to describe the activities of the family have distorted our temporal perspective. "He, she, all of them" are in their graves; only the final line of each stanza takes place in the present. This distortion serves both to heighten the contrast between the living and the dead and to illustrate the universality of death.

As we have seen, "During Wind and Rain" is organized in such a way that we must infer a temporal order if we are to respond to the tone of the poem. The organization of the following poem asks us to infer certain spatial relationships as we read it.

The Most of It

He thought he kept the universe alone;
For all the voice in answer he could wake
Was but the mocking echo of his own
From some tree-hidden cliff across the lake.
Some morning from the boulder-broken beach   5
He would cry out on life, that what it wants
Is not its own love back in copy speech,
But counter-love, original response.
And nothing ever came of what he cried
Unless it was the embodiment that crashed   10
In the cliff's talus on the other side,
And then in the far distant water splashed.
But after a time allowed for it to swim,
Instead of proving human when it neared
And someone else additional to him,   15

As a great buck it powerfully appeared,
Pushing the crumpled water up ahead,
And landed pouring like a waterfall,
And stumbled through the rocks with horny tread,
And forced the underbrush—and that was all.   20

R. Frost

As soon as we learn, in the first line of the poem, that the speaker "thought he kept the universe alone," we become conscious of his relationship, psychological as well as spatial, to everything outside himself. He is uneasy about the gulf that seems to separate him from the external world and recognizes that the only way such a gulf can be traversed is by "love": a need to be united with the other. He declares his need to nature and then awaits from it some "counter-love," some "original response" that might convince him that nature and all its forces were not entirely indifferent to him. The subject of the poem is thus the speaker's need for some kind of unity with the external world, and the function of the poem's organization is to evoke the spatial relationship between the speaker and nature, to evoke it in such a way that its psychological corollary is made more immediate for us.

In order to respond to the organization of the poem, we need only imagine the relationship that exists between any "here" and any other "there." Once we have done this, however, we must be careful to notice the development that this spatial relationship undergoes within the structure of the poem. The first four lines represent the distance between himself and nature.

He thought he kept the universe alone;
For all the voice in answer he could wake
Was but the mocking echo of his own
From some tree-hidden cliff across the lake.

In line 2, his voice goes from here to there. From there to here comes only an echo. Lines 5 through 9 reinforce our sense of the spatial relationship.

Some morning from the boulder-broken beach
He would cry out on life, that what it wants

Is not its own love back in copy speech,
But counter-love, original response.
And nothing ever came of what he cried . . .

The poet repeats the organizational formula of the first four lines: from here to there goes the "cry"; from there to here comes "nothing." And since these five lines also provide detailed information about his motives for wanting to narrow the distance between himself and nature, we might almost say that "nothing" happens in the remainder of the poem. For if we consider it only in terms of what he sought, the second half of the poem is essentially anticlimactic. The "embodiment that crashed/ In the cliff's talus on the other side" conforms no more closely to what the poet sought than did the "mocking echo of his own" voice. In terms of its structural development, then, the poem ends immediately before the "unless" clause in line 10.

Or does it? The second half of the poem amplifies the "unless" in a very vivid way. Much of this vividness depends upon our inferring the spatial relationship between the speaker and nature, the here and there, as it is suddenly and inscrutably affected by the appearance, approach, and disappearance of the buck. Before the buck appears, this relationship is virtually static but serves, nonetheless, to delineate the here and there. Had they not been delineated, the significance to the poet of the buck would be much less intelligible to us. Until he experiences the very real, active "original response" that the buck provides, his relationship with the there is still incomplete. That the last eleven lines of the poem can be relegated to an "unless" clause is testimony enough that the buck offers no greater satisfaction to the poet than did his own echo; he still knows that he is isolated in a universe that is totally indifferent to his existence. But because the here-there relationship is the organizational principle, the definition is not resolved until the poet has had an answer from nature.

As we have seen, "During Wind and Rain" is organized in such a way that we must recognize in it two separate series of temporal associations, one having to do with the four seasons, the other with successive stages in the maturation of a family. "The Most of It" elicits a much simpler association, asking us to imagine only two separate points and then remain sensitive to the dynamics of their relationship as it is developed throughout the poem. In order to apprehend the relationships between the various parts in both poems, we are asked to make associations with categories that are objective in nature. We regard time and space as being more susceptible to precise measurement than more subjective categories, such as love. The terms we use in measuring the length of time between one's ninth and fourteenth birthdays may in fact be no more stable than those we might use to measure degrees of love. But we are nonetheless much more likely to agree on the precise nature of a quantity such as a year or a mile than on the nature of a quality such as romantic love or a fear of death, which cannot be dissociated from the particular emotions that it assumes within each individual's experience.

The structure of the next poem is in part implicit. If we are to recognize how it functions, we must make associations that are decidedly more subjective than those evoked by the last two poems we have considered.

On My First Son

Farewell, thou child of my right hand and joy;
My sin was too much hope of thee, loved boy.
Seven years thou wert lent to me, and I thee pay,
Exacted by thy fate, on the just day.
O, could I lose all Father now. For why   5
Will man lament the state he should envy?
To have so soon 'scaped world's and flesh's rage,
And, if no other misery, yet age?
Rest in soft peace, and asked, say here doth lie
Ben Jonson his best piece of poetry.   10
For whose sake, henceforth, all his vows be such
As what he loves may never like too much.

Ben Jonson's epitaph on his son is the argument of a stoic. It describes the poet's attempt to adjust his grief over the loss of his son to a more rational understanding of the situation; an understanding that he hopes will enable him to avoid such an extremity of grief in the future. But the experience that the poem defines has to do as much with Jonson the father as with Jonson the stoic. The epitaph itself, finally, is a composite of rational self-instruction and emotional resistance to that instruction; to say this is to say enough about the general nature of Jonson's experience in losing his son. But if we are to appreciate the precision with which Jonson has defined the experience, we must pay careful attention to the way the organization develops the relationship between Jonson's stoicism and his feelings as a father.

The poem is written in couplets (two successive lines that end with rhyming words: "joy" and "boy," "pay" and "day," for example). Stoicism is central to the first, second, fourth, and sixth couplets, while the third and fifth are more expressive of his feelings as a father. In strictly numerical terms, then, stoicism is the more prevalent of the two sides of Jonson's response to his loss. In the eight stoical lines Jonson argues logically, and the transitions both to these lines and within them are explicit. The four lines that are more representative of the father in Jonson are quite different in structure; they are not argumentative, and the transitions into them are implicit and require of us associations so subjective that they almost contradict what is argued in the stoical lines. Although it is decidedly the function of the poem's structure to unite Jonson's contradictory responses, we cannot understand the work that the structure does until we look at each element separately and define more carefully the conflict between them.

Jonson defines two quite separate motives for his stoicism. Although they also reflect his fatherly emotions, lines 5 through 8 tell us explicitly that it is irrational to mourn over the boy's death. Because his son has escaped the pains of this world at such an early age, the boy's present "state," in death, should be envied rather than lamented. The second motive is perhaps less obvious but certainly no less relevant. Jonson tells us that if he is to understand the causes of his son's death he must recognize that the child was never in any true sense his own; the "sin" to which he refers in line 2 is that he had forgotten that the boy belonged only to God. The death has reminded him very painfully of his proper relationship to his son: The child was merely "lent" to him, and God could "justly" demand the repayment of the loan at any time.

It is in line 5 that we encounter the lament itself, and it is important to recognize the nature of the transition from line 4 to line

5. This transition is not logical, but is rather an associative reaction to the preceding argument that God could in justice do anything He pleased with the boy; the father in Jonson responds violently to this notion. As we move into the fourth couplet the transition is again logical. And after he has described what is enviable about the state of death in lines 7 and 8, Jonson returns, in lines 9 and 10, to a statement that represents his grief, a statement that can be regarded only as irrational when considered within the context of the poem.

For despite his earlier references to his "sin" of "too much hope" for his son, despite his understanding that the boy was never truly his, Jonson addresses his son directly in lines 9 and 10 and tells him to be prepared to tell anyone who asks that he was the best thing his father ever made. While the sense of these lines does not directly contradict lines 2, 3, and 4, it definitely emphasizes Jonson's awareness of his claim to the boy and explicitly indicates his resistance to a purely rational resignation to his son's death. For Jonson to suggest a logical contradiction with lines 2 through 4 is indeed to take a risk. But logic is hardly his concern at this point in the poem. His concern is rather the uniqueness and intensity of his relationship with his son, and to represent this concern he must take risks. To address his son directly and pretend that someone is likely to ask the boy for his credentials, to label him a poem, and to name himself explicitly is to strain the decorum established by the straightforward exposition of the preceding lines. But lines 9 and 10 do not break the decorum. Instead, they extend the tonal limits of the poem in direct conformity to Jonson's emotional dilemma. If we are to learn precisely what is involved in the poet's concluding vow, we must be able to recognize the precise extent to which stoical consolation remains for Jonson unconsoling.

Although the final couplet bears greater resemblance to the "rational" than to the "irrational" lines of the poem, we will miss the nature of the distinction between "love" and "like" if we assume that the vow is spoken any less by the father than by the stoic. It is true that Jonson censures the selfishness that necessarily accompanies being "too much" the father. To love as he should love, he must be ready to concede his expectation that the loved one remain bound within mortality. And yet his relationship with the dead boy has been so uniquely personal that it is ultimately only for his son's sake that he makes the vow. It is a vow that is motivated at once by a stoic's resignation to a "just" world order and this particular father's resentment of that order. Much of the clarity of Jonson's poem is due to its structure. The dilemma that he experiences in responding to his son's death is intelligible to us only because the transitions to the "irrational" lines are able to imply so effectively why a strictly rational response is an incomplete response.

I would like to consider one more poem in this chapter. Its structure, like that of Jonson's, relies heavily on our ability to make subjective associations.

To Autumn

Season of mists and mellow fruitfulness!
  Close bosom-friend of the maturing sun;
Conspiring with him how to load and bless
  With fruit the vines that round the thatch-eaves run;
To bend with apples the mossed cottage-trees   5
  And fill all fruit with ripeness to the core;
    To swell the gourd, and plump the hazel shells
With a sweet kernel; to set budding more,
  And still more, later flowers for the bees,
  Until they think warm days will never cease,   10
    For summer has o'er-brimmed their clammy cells.

Who hath not seen thee oft amid thy store?
  Sometimes whoever seeks abroad may find
Thee sitting careless on a granary floor,
  Thy hair soft-lifted by the winnowing wind;   15
Or on a half-reaped furrow sound asleep,
  Drowsed with the fume of poppies, while thy hook
    Spares the next swath and all its twinéd flowers;
And sometimes like a gleaner thou dost keep
  Steady thy laden head across a brook;   20
  Or by a cider-press, with patient look,
    Thou watchest the last oozings, hours by hours.

Where are the songs of Spring? Ay, where are they?
  Think not of them, thou hast thy music too,
While barréd clouds bloom the soft-dying day,   25
  And touch the stubble-plains with rosy hue;

> Then in a wailful choir the small gnats mourn
>   Among the river sallows, borne aloft
>   Or sinking as the light wind lives or dies;
> And full-grown lambs loud bleat from hilly bourn;   30
>   Hedge-crickets sing; and now with treble soft
>   The redbreast whistles from a garden-croft,
>   And gathering swallows twitter in the skies.

The subject of the poem resembles that of "The Most of It" in one important respect: Both poets exhibit a need to be united with the landscape. In this poem, however, no cry is issued by the speaker, no "counter-love" from nature requested. Instead, the autumn landscape is for two stanzas quietly personified in such a way that we are almost lulled into believing that counter-love might indeed be forthcoming from it. Autumn is characterized as a friend of the sun and capable of delightful conspiracies that result in fertility for the entire pastoral landscape. The personification of autumn is at its most intense in the second stanza. There, not only are a variety of human traits attributed to autumn—"sitting careless," "hair," "sound asleep," "laden head," "patient look," etc.—but the stanza itself is addressed directly to the personification of autumn and thus implies, more strongly than the first stanza, the possibility of some kind of dialogue between the poet and the landscape.

After the second line of the final stanza, on the other hand, the poem is quite noticeably free of personification, and it concludes with descriptions of a redbreast, lambs, hedge-crickets, and swallows that are almost as absent of personification as the buck in "The Most of It." Clearly, then, the structure of the poem is such that an intimate communion with nature is suggested in the middle stanza and more or less ignored in the final one. There is nothing in the poem that explains this very important shift of direction to us. But the details that describe the landscape are handled with so much control that we can infer the precise reasons for this shift. Just as in "During Wind and Rain," associations with the passing of time are central to our ability to apprehend the relationships between the parts of the poem. But in "To Autumn," these temporal associations undergo a much more complicated development than in "During Wind and Rain."

In the first stanza, all of the details describe the abundance and the beauty of autumn. The gourd, apples, hazel shells, and flowers are so ripe and so numerous that there is no hint of the sterile winter that will follow. There seems to be so much of summer in the beauty of autumn that the bees "think warm days will never cease." Throughout the stanza there is the suggestion that it is precisely the continuance and the fruition of summer that make autumn so beautiful that we want to commune with it in a personal way. But of course fruition must also imply death. The "maturing sun" is a vital element in the fertility that is autumn, but so too is the simple passage of time. The time of harvest is a time of life, for what is harvested is full of life; but harvest takes place in anticipation of winter—the season of death. Whatever remnants of summer there may be in autumn are dispersed as soon as the harvest itself is completed. Thus, the first stanza asks us to associate the present season with the one that has immediately preceded it; to think back in time. But the poet is aware that simply thinking back cannot alter the nature of time, and so the allusions to summer are discontinued in the second stanza.

We are not asked, however, to think ahead to future seasons in the second stanza. Instead, we are asked not to think in temporal terms at all. Because the completed harvest means the death of what is harvested and presages the winter, the second stanza shows us autumn "amid" the mature and abundant produce. References to the produce itself intimate the passing of time, but the implication of these references is neutralized by references to autumn in a state of torpor that will not permit the work to be concluded. We are referred to the "granary floor." But instead of finding the final harvesting busily underway, we find autumn "sitting careless." Two lines later we find her "on a half-reaped furrow sound asleep," and the harvesting is suspended as her "hook/ Spares the next swath and all its twinéd flowers." In the midst of all her plenty, then, autumn causes us to think neither back to the summer nor forward to the winter. What her personification implies is this: If we do in fact commune with autumn as with a beloved person, we will experience the same sense of timelessness that she is characterized as having. There is work to be done at harvest time. One cannot afford always to be "Drowsed with the fume of poppies," but must "sometimes" have the "steady" and "laden head" that is required of the gleaner as she cautiously crosses the brook with her produce. And yet, to reverse the cliché, time is hardly of the essence. There is time, in autumn, to watch the "last oozings" of the cider-press "hours by hours."

The first stanza stresses autumn's relationship to summertime and implies that it is this relationship that lends so much beauty to autumn. With her hair "soft-lifted by the winnowing wind" in the second stanza, autumn is beautiful because the season seems to be outside of time. In neither stanza are we referred directly to any time in the future. But notice how the final stanza begins: "Where are the songs of spring? Ay, where are they?" The question is asked, and repeated, because the inevitability of winter is an implicit characteristic of autumn. The "songs of spring," the answer must come, are another season away; and that season is the one that makes us think more immediately than any of the others about where time finally takes us—to death. Winter is the death of the year. It is the end of a seasonal cycle that will not, for those who die, be repeated. The fertile abundance that comes in autumn may tempt us to believe, with the bees, that "warm days will never cease." Or it may lull us into forgetting about time altogether. But once the fields have been harvested and there remain only the "stubble-plains," autumn must be seen in its very real temporal context. Autumn is no less related to winter than to summer. Death is subtly implied in the references to "the soft-dying day" and the "wailful choir" of gnats, "borne aloft/ Or sinking as the light wind lives or dies"—like all of us who are subject to the whims of time. The lambs who were newly born and small in spring and early summer are now "full-grown," aging. And the swallows are now gathering—soon, perhaps, to migrate to the warmer climates of the south.

But although "the songs of spring" mark the beginning of a new cycle of the seasons and betoken birth rather than death, autumn is advocated to "think not of them." For despite autumn's unmistakable implications of death, its own music is no less beautiful than spring's, and the descriptive details of the third stanza do much to reflect this beauty. Autumn is beautiful no less because it is *like* summertime or like no time than because it *is* itself. To disguise any of the reality of autumn by pretending that it is something it is not is to miss its very particular beauty. Whatever our desires to the contrary, however much its beauty may motivate us to think it so, autumn is not a person. Neither is it summer, although it may remind us strongly of summer. Neither is it out of time. In order for us to apprehend precisely why autumn is beautiful to the speaker of the poem, we must be able to see the same kinds of relationships between autumn and time that he sees. Each stanza qualifies the relationship that is implied in the previous stanza, and the progression of the poem mirrors—in a very simple way—the progression of autumn from Indian summer to the peak of the harvesting to its transition into winter. But as we have seen, it is the more particular implications of each of these stages that the highly complicated structure of the poem supports. Within each stanza, the transitions from word to word, phrase to phrase, and sentence to sentence are controlled in such a way that we can infer what these transitions imply.

These are precisely the kinds of inferences we have made in considering each of the last four poems in this chapter. In "Church Monuments" and "In Time of Plague," remember, we were not asked to infer such transitions but were instead provided with explicit connectives between the parts of the poem. But the subjects of "During Wind and Rain," "The Most of It," "On My First Son," and "To Autumn" have each necessitated a structure that is at least partially implicit. Had any of these four poems provided explicit signposts for every transition, our attention would have been wrenched away from the subject itself. Imagine how disturbing it would be to have the poet tell you, in "To Autumn," that autumn will not be personified as extensively in the third stanza as in the second since we ought to think of autumn as it really is and not as a beautiful woman.

On the other hand, imagine how much more diffuse and random and how much less insistent "Church Monuments" and "In Time of Plague" would be if we were expected to proceed through their arguments in any less explicit a way than we do. Neither poet wants to leave open to our private associations with his subject the possibility that we respond to death in any other way than the one he describes. "During Wind and Rain" and "On My First Son" employ a more equal proportion of explicit and implicit transitions than any of the other four poems. But regardless of the differences in the kind of structure used, each poet that we have discussed has (1) chosen the particular organizational procedure that was most appropriate to his own particular responses to his subjects and (2) controlled that procedure in such a way that we can learn more about his responses than we could if we ignored the structure of the poem.

The organization and diction of a poem are completely dependent upon one another, and you should not be troubled if your first attempts to sort out the two elements are not successful. The distinction between the two is a real one, and you will soon begin to discover it for yourself. You will see that organization resides not so much in the words themselves as in the transitions that separate words, clauses, sentences, and stanzas from one another. When the poet is in control of his medium, these transitions are decidedly meaningful. If the transitions from part to part are explicit, you are obliged not only to apprehend them but to check to see whether implicit transitions are also operating. If the transitions are the implicit, more silent kind, you must try to recognize their precise function by making only those associations that the parts seem to prompt when taken collectively and in sequence. It is an important part of your job as reader to discover what the structure of a poem tells you both about the parts it organizes and about the whole.

meter and rhythm

Reading poetry is a very special kind of reading. Until you are able to hear the poem, even when reading to yourself, you are dealing with something other than poetry. Read the following poem aloud to yourself. As you do so, try to listen to its *rhythm* by reducing to a minimum any impulse you might have to give certain syllables more emphasis than they receive naturally.

Under the mountain, as when first I knew
Its low black roof and chimney creeper-twined,
The red house stands; and yet my footsteps find,
Vague in the walks, waste balm and feverfew.
But they are gone: no soft-eyed sisters trip   5
Across the porch or lintels; where, behind,
The mother sat, sat knitting with pursed lip.
The house stands vacant in its green recess,

Absent of beauty as a broken heart.
The wild rain enters, and the sunset wind   10
Sighs in the chambers of their loveliness
Or shakes the pane—and in the silent noons
The glass falls from the window, part by part,
And ringeth faintly in the grassy stones.

As you read, you should be able to hear that the pitch, duration, and vowel and consonant sounds differ in each syllable (except for the several repeated syllables: "as," "and," "sat," etc.). Let's describe these differences between the sounds of certain syllables as differences of *stress*. The poet wants us to hear the unique sound each syllable makes as it contributes to the highly particular rhythm of the poem. When we read the first phrase of this poem, the poet wants us to be able to discern that the first syllable of "mountain" is the most heavily stressed syllable in the phrase, and that the first syllable of "under" is more heavily stressed than the three remaining syllables.

At the same time that we listen to the poem's rhythm, the poet expects us to recognize the general pattern of sound in the poem—its *meter*. To do this we must temporarily ignore the differences between the syllables and try to see what they have in common. When we have found these similarities, we will call them not stresses—a term we have reserved for discussing the differences between syllables—but *accents*.

To discover its metrical pattern, we will scan the poem. *Scansion* is nothing more than a method of indicating the kind of pattern that operates in a poem. The unit that we deal with is the line:

1 2 3   4 5 6 7   8 9 10
Under the mountain, as when first I knew

After counting the syllables in a line, you have to decide how many feet that line contains. A *foot* is a group of either two or three syllables. Feet of two syllables are by far the more common, and so you should always begin by dividing a line into consecutive groups of two syllables. But the division of a line into feet will always have an element of trial and error about it. Sometimes your impulse to play the percentages by dividing the line into disyllabic feet will betray you. If it does, though, you will quickly discover your error, and it will be a relatively easy matter to redivide the line into trisyllabic feet. In this particular line, each foot *is* comprised of two syllables.

Under | the moun | tain, as | when first | I knew

After you have divided the line into its proper feet, you can focus your attention directly on each foot and try to determine which syllable within the foot is more heavily stressed. In the first foot of this line, the first syllable receives greater stress than the second, and so they scan respectively as an accented and an unaccented syllable. In each of the remaining feet of the line, the second syllable is the more heavily stressed. Each of these feet, then, scans as an unaccented and an accented syllable respectively. The various kinds of feet that you might encounter in any given poem are these:

Iamb: unaccented syllable, accented syllable (or ⌣′).
Trochee: accented syllable, unaccented syllable (′⌣).
Anapest: unaccented syllable, unaccented syllable, accented syllable (⌣⌣′).
Dactyl: accented syllable, unaccented syllable, unaccented syllable (′⌣⌣).

The first line of the poem can be described in this way:

Trochee, iamb, iamb, iamb, iamb

or

′⌣ | ⌣′ | ⌣′ | ⌣′ | ⌣′

Since the meter of the poem is the general pattern of accented syllables that the reader is led to expect throughout the poem, we might very well anticipate that the second line will scan identically with the first. But it does not.

Its low | black roof | and chim | ney creep | er-twined,

The line is a series of five iambs. So, too, is line 3.

The red | house stands; | and yet | my foot | steps find,

By this point in the poem we can be fairly certain that the general metrical pattern of the poem is five iambs in each line. The following terminology describes the number of feet in each line of any poem:

> Monometer: one foot
> Dimeter: two feet
> Trimeter: three feet
> Tetrameter: four feet
> Pentameter: five feet
> Hexameter: six feet
> Fourteener: seven feet

Since most of the lines of the poem we have been discussing contain five iambs, we describe its metrical pattern as iambic pentameter. When we scan the poem, we must remember to be aware of each individual foot. But the general metrical pattern of this poem—iambic pentameter—is not overthrown by the presence of trochees in the first foot of lines 4, 9, and 11 and the second foot of line 13.

Iambic pentameter is the most common metrical form in English verse, but you will meet several others. There is iambic tetrameter:

> Hăd wé | bŭt wórld | ĕnoúgh, | ănd tíme,
> Thĭs cóy | nĕss, lád | ў, wére | nŏ críme.

Iambic trimeter:

> Ădíeu, | fărewéll | eárth's blíss,
> Thĭs wórld | ŭncér | taĭn ís;

Iambic dimeter:

> Ĭ thée | ădvíse
> Ĭf thóu | bĕ wíse
> Tŏ keép | thў wít
> Thŏugh ĭt | bĕ smáll:

Even iambic monometer:

> Thŭs Í
> Păss bý
> Ănd díe:

Trochaic tetrameter:

> Kiss me, | sweet: the | wary | lover
>
> Can your | favors | keep, and | cover,

You may also encounter meters that are based on feet having three syllables, such as this one in anapestic tetrameter:

> The Assyr | ian came down | like the wolf | on the fold,
>
> And his co | horts were gleam | ing in pur | ple and gold;
>
> And the sheen | of their spears | was like stars | on the sea,
>
> When the blue | waves roll gent | ly on deep | Galilee.

But lines that are basically anapestic or dactylic are mixed, more frequently than not, with other kinds of feet. The scansion of lines whose meters are *mixed* can be a very complicated matter. The following lines, for example, are essentially dactylic, but it is a very incomplete description of them to say simply that they're dactylic lines.

> What if a | day, or a | month, or a | year
>
> Crown thy de | lights with a | thousand | sweet con | tentings?
>
> Cannot a | chance of a | night or an | hour
>
> Cross thy de | sires with as | many | sad tor | mentings?

The meter is mixed not only within individual lines, but also from line to line; the first and third lines scan identically, as do the second and fourth. Lines 2 and 4 scan as two dactyls and three trochees. But notice what we have in lines 1 and 3. The lines begin with three dactyls and conclude with a single, heavily stressed syllable. This syllable is best described as an *extrametrical syllable;* its presence in the line does not disrupt the metrical pattern of the line itself. Heavily or lightly stressed syllables may be added to any line. A lightly stressed one is common enough at the end of a line and is referred to as a *feminine ending.* Heavily stressed extrametrical syllables, however, are so rare that you should be wary about finding them. With that advice in mind, of course, you can claim that lines 1 and 3 should scan as two dactyls, a trochee, and an iamb; and such a scansion would be an accurate description of the meter of the line.

But a second piece of advice must take precedence here: as long as it does not provide a distorted representation of the meter itself, your description of the meter of a line should always be as simple as possible.

Learning how to describe the meter of a poem is a simple thing, for it involves very few considerations. It will be difficult only if you forget the distinction between meter and rhythm. Meter is really little more than an oversimplification of rhythm; although you can recognize the rhythm of a poem only by remaining sensitive to the immense variety of sounds that make up the poem, you come to know the meter of that poem by being temporarily dull to this variety. To discover the metrical pattern of a poem you must decide only the kinds and number of feet in each of its lines; and as you have already seen, your choices in this matter are extremely limited. Meter isn't so simple a proposition that you will never make mistakes in trying to define it accurately, but within a short time you should usually be able to spot even the most complicated kinds of metrical patterns.

Although you should always observe a distinction between meter and rhythm, you should not forget that the two do coincide in one important way. Suppose, for example, that you had been asked to scan the following line after learning that iambic pentameter is the most common metrical pattern in the language:

What if a day, or a month, or a year

Since the line has ten syllables, it would be reasonable for you to want to scan the line in this way:

Whăt íf | ă dáy, | or ă | mŏnth, ór | ă yéar

As we have already seen, this scansion would be wrong. It has done much more than oversimplify the way each syllable sounds within its own foot; it has distorted that sound. Unless you read a line aloud to yourself as naturally as you can, unless you remain sensitive to the way that line really sounds, you will often scan it incorrectly.

But correct scansion never ensures your hearing the poem correctly, and this is why it is important not to confuse meter and rhythm. "Under the mountain, as when first I knew" is a line that appears in an iambic pentameter poem. Still, if you do not notice more particularly that the first foot of the line is a trochee, you will be missing an important rhythmic feature. As we have seen, the poet has substituted another kind of foot for the one that exists in the metrical pattern. Were there no such altering, poetry would be a very dull business. General patterns of sound would be all that concern us, and the number of patterns would long ago have been exhausted. When we read poetry, however, we are concerned with much more than general patterns of sound. We are concerned with particular poems, and one element of a poem's particularity is its inimitable rhythm. Let us try to focus, now, on some of the other features that contribute to the rhythm of the poem.

While substitutions cause a line to vary from its metrical pattern, they can still be described in metrical terms. In trying to spot a substitution, you are still dealing with the metrical category of accent rather than with the rhythmical category of stress. There is thus a sense in which substitutions are a metrical, and not a rhythmical, concern. The term *variation*, on the other hand, applies exclusively to the rhythm of the line. This term is intended as a reminder that every syllable varies in its degree of stress from every other. The seventh line of our poem is a fine illustration of the difference between meter and rhythm, accent and stress.

The moth | ĕr sát, | sắt knít | tíng wíth | pursed líp.

The syllable "sat" appears twice in the line. Rhythmically, the value of that syllable is identical in both instances. Metrically, though, its value contrasts absolutely; in the first instance it is an accented syllable, whereas in the second it is not. When you read the line aloud, you will read it very badly if you allow accent, rather than stress, to be your guide. All accented syllables do not really sound alike; neither do all unaccented syllables. This fact can be referred to with the catch-all term *variation*.

If we say that the meter of a line is iambic pentameter and its rhythm includes several variations, we aren't really being very precise. Such a description will apply to every line of iambic pentameter verse in the language. If the term *variation* is to be used meaningfully, therefore, it must be accompanied by a more detailed account of the variations in stress from syllable to syllable within the line.

Statements about rhythmical variation can thus become lengthy affairs. Let's try a very limited description of the variations in the seventh line,

The mother sat, sat knitting with pursed lip.
1   2   3   4   5   6   7   8   9   10

We would begin by saying that the rhythm of the first four syllables conforms very closely to the meter. What this means is that there is relatively little variation in the degree of stress of the first and third syllables; and that, similarly, the second and fourth syllables receive approximately equal stress. The rhythm of the remainder of the line, however, varies noticeably from the meter. As we have seen, the fifth syllable receives almost precisely the same stress as the fourth, but it is unaccented. Rhythmically, then, the fourth, fifth, and sixth syllables are all heavily stressed, despite the fact that they are regular enough metrically. The seventh and eighth syllables are both so lightly stressed that it is difficult to assign their appropriate metrical values. Remember that every foot of verse, whether it is made up of two or three syllables, has one and only one accented syllable; when the reader scans the poem, he is therefore forced to decide which of the two syllables is the more heavily stressed. Although I am tempted to scan the fourth foot of the line as a trochee, I think it is more properly scanned as an iamb. But regardless of the proper scansion of these syllables, our ear should tell us that the unaccented syllables of both adjoining feet—"sat" and "pursed"—are stressed much more heavily than either syllable in this foot. Scansion is always incidental to the way a line sounds. Whereas the meter of the line presents us with an abstract pattern that scans like this:

ᵕ/ | ᵕ/ | ᵕ/ | ᵕ/ | ᵕ/

we hear the rhythm of the line more particularly in the degree of stress each syllable receives. Thus:

Light, heavy, light, heavy, heavy, heavy, light, light,
heavy, heavy.

Breaking down the rhythm of the line as we have just done tells us more about the line than scansion tells us, but it is still only a very approximate description. Saying that the syllables are either heavily or lightly stressed greatly oversimplifies the wide variety of degrees of stress. Rhythmically, every syllable varies from every other, the only exception being the syllable that is repeated. It is really impossible, therefore, to describe precisely the way a line sounds.

But there are further difficulties in trying to speak accurately about the way a given line sounds. So far, we've been considering the relationships of single syllables to one another. We must now look at them as they come together into grammatical units. For the rhythm of a line depends as much on the way groups of syllables relate to one another as on the more basic issue that we have already examined.

It is easy to see how really artificial meter is when we realize that phrases as well as single words do not always conform to metrical feet. For example, in the first line of the poem,

> Under the mountain,‖as when first I knew

the first phrase ends in the middle of the third foot.

The metrical term for the pause that you make after completing this phrase is *caesura*. As with all terms that apply to the meter of a line, to speak of the caesura of a line is to oversimplify the way that line sounds. Just as there is always and only one accented syllable in each foot, so there is always and only one caesura in each line. No matter how imperceptible the pause within a given line may be, the caesura, by definition, never falls at the end of a line. Finding the caesura tells you very little about the rhythm of the line. In the eighth line,

> The house stands vacant‖in its green recess,

the caesura falls in the same place that it does in the first line, but you pause for a much shorter time when reading this line than you do when reading the first. Neither does the caesura of a line tell you anything about the location or duration of secondary pauses, such as the one after the eighth syllable in line 6.

> Across the porch or lintels;‖where, behind

The syntax contributes significantly to the rhythm of a poem in that it determines the location and duration of the pauses in each of the lines. Just as significantly, the syntax influences the movement of the poem from one line to another. Metrically, you are concerned exclusively with the line as an absolute and independent entity. Rhythmically, on the other hand, you must see that each line has a necessary relationship to its adjoining lines. Punctuation is often of some help in showing how a transition from one line to another should sound. Clearly, the period at the end of line 4,

> Vague in the walks, waste balm and feverfew.

enforces a full pause. Here, as with every line in the poem that concludes with a period, we feel no tendency to read straight through to the next line. In the lines concluding with commas, the time that we pause will vary more from instance to instance, but the punctuation still guides the length of our pauses.

But notice the *run-on* lines—the lines that conclude with no punctuation whatever. In every case, the duration of our pause at the end of the run-on line differs. You must try to be sensitive to these differences; it will help you to notice a few of the factors responsible for them. The most rapid run-on in the poem is the one from line 5 to line 6. What this means, very simply, is that you pause for a shorter time after line 5 than after any other line in the poem.

> But they are gone: no soft-eyed sisters trip
> Across the porch or lintels; where, behind,

When we compare the syntax, sense, and rhythm of this run-on with that of the others, we begin to see why our pause after line 10 must be relatively short. Line 5 concludes with a verb, and is followed immediately, in line 6, with a preposition that continues the action of that verb. Not only do we anticipate hearing about where and how the girls tripped, but the skip from one line to the next is so imitative of the act being described that we are tempted to speed the transition even more. Of the other lines that do not conclude with punctuation, only one has so basic a grammatical relationship between its final word and the first word of the following line. Lines 2, 12, and 13 begin with a word whose relationship to the word immediately preceding it is less intimate than what we have with "trip/ Across."

> Under the mountain, as when first I knew
> Its low black roof and chimney creeper-twined,
>
> (lines 1–2)

> Sighs in the chambers of their loveliness
> Or shakes the pane—and in the silent noons
> The glass falls from the window, part by part,
>
> (lines 11–13)

In reading these lines, one is thus able to pause for a slightly longer time at the end of each than at the end of line 5. The syntax of lines 10 and 11, however, occasions a more rapid run-on.

> The wild rain enters, and the sunset wind
> Sighs in the chambers of their loveliness

The speed with which this run-on is read is very close to that of lines 5 and 6. Were we concerned only with syntax, I suppose that "wind/ Sighs" would have to be read in as close a conjunction with one another as would "trip/ Across . . ." Line 10 concludes with the subject of the clause, and we are thus awaiting the arrival of the verb. But the rhythm of the lines is also a factor in the rapidity of the run-on. In the first foot of line 11, a trochee has been substituted for the iamb that the metrical pattern of the poem has led us to expect. In a sense we are thus thrown from the heavily stressed syllable concluding line 10 to another heavily stressed syllable in the next line. This tends to slow down the movement from syllable to syllable. When we move from line 5 to line 6, however, we encounter no substitution.

> But they are gone: no soft-eyed sisters trip
> Across the porch or lintels;

There will be a very strong tendency here for you to read the division between the lines with no longer pause than if "trip across" appeared within the same iambic line.

We have talked enough, now, about what meter and rhythm are, and it is time to ask why they have deserved so much of our attention. There is perhaps no more difficult question to be asked about the nature of poetry, and the answers to it can only be approximate. The easiest answer is that poetry is derived from song, and that its musical derivations have been preserved in the care which the poet devotes to the sound of his poem. But if this answer is at all helpful, it prompts a still more difficult question: Is the sound of a poem relevant to what its words tell us? The answer must be that if it is not there is something wrong with the poem. The meter and rhythm of any poem should be the meter and rhythm best suited to the poet's subject. In the following poem, for example, the poet is attempting to convince himself that his reason should control his emotion, and the regularity and stiffness with which the poem moves seem to correspond perfectly with the subject.

Gascoigne's Lullaby

Sing lullaby, as women do,
Wherewith they bring their babes to rest,
And lullaby can I sing too
As womanly as can the best.
With lullaby they still the child,   5
And if I be not much beguiled,
Full many wanton babes have I
Which must be stilled with lullaby.

First lullaby my youthful years;
It is now time to go to bed,   10
For crooked age and hoary hairs
Have won the haven within my head.
With lullaby, then, youth be still;
With lullaby content thy will;
Since courage quails and comes behind,   15
Go sleep, and so beguile thy mind.

Next, lullaby my gazing eyes,
Which wonted were to glance apace.
For every glass may now suffice
To show the furrows in my face;   20
With lullaby then wink awhile,
With lullaby your looks beguile;

Let no fair face nor beauty bright
Entice you eft with vain delight.

And lullaby, my wanton will;   25
Let reason's rule now reign thy thought,
Since all too late I find by skill
How dear I have thy fancies bought;
With lullaby now take thine ease,
With lullaby thy doubts appease.   30
For trust to this: if thou be still,
My body shall obey thy will.

Eke lullaby, my loving boy,
My little Robin, take thy rest;
Since age is cold and nothing coy,   35
Keep close thy coin, for so is best;
With lullaby be thou content,
With lullaby thy lusts relent,
Let others pay which hath mo pence;
Thou art too poor for such expense.   40

Thus lullaby, my youth, mine eyes,
My will, my ware, and all that was.
I can no more delays devise,
But welcome pain, let pleasure pass;
With lullaby now take your leave,   45
With lullaby your dreams deceive;
And when you rise with waking eye,
Remember then this lullaby.

The expectations that the meter creates in us from the beginning are
confirmed throughout the poem. The iambic tetrameter in eight-line
stanzas is rhymed *ababccdd*. In the rather long poem there are no
substitutions whatever, and the lines are consistently end-stopped.
Nor are there more than a few noticeable variations in the degree of
stress received by accented and unaccented syllables. So regularly
does the caesura fall after the second foot that when it does not—as
in the last line of stanza two—it calls considerable attention to itself.
The poet senses that he is aging and that it is time to mend his ways.

The lullaby is designed to quiet his more worldly impulses, and the effect of the poem's movement is to realize the lull itself.

Imagine, for the moment, that the subject of the poem above had been cast in a metrical form such as this:

The Night Piece, to Julia

Her eyes the glowworm lend thee;
The shooting stars attend thee;
   And the elves also,
   Whose little eyes glow,
Like the sparks of fire, befriend thee.   5

No will-o'-the-wisp mislight thee;
Nor snake, or slowworm bite thee.
   But on, on thy way,
   Not making a stay,
Since ghost there's none to affright thee.   10

Let not the dark thee cumber;
What though the moon does slumber?
   The stars of the night
   Will lend thee their light,
Like tapers clear without number.   15

Then, Julia, let me woo thee,
Thus, thus to come unto me.
   And when I shall meet
   Thy silvery feet,
My soul I'll pour into thee.   20

Such flexibility and grace would be very inappropriate in a poem which specifically renounces beauty. But considering the fact that the poet's subject in this poem is his desire for Julia, the meter and rhythm of the poem could hardly be improved. Again, the poem is written in stanzas; this stanzaic form, though, is a considerably more delicate affair. The first, second, and fifth lines are iambic trimeter, concluding with a feminine ending. The third and fourth lines scan as an iamb and then an anapest, although this order is reversed in line 3:

And the elves | also,

The rhyme scheme of the stanza is *aabba*, which in itself is not particularly unique; but in conjunction with the alternating seven- and five-syllable lines, the rhyme is a lovely one. The poem has numerous substitutions, and throughout there is much variety in the degree to which unaccented and accented syllables are stressed. Despite the fact that Julia herself is never described explicitly, we come away from the poem with a very distinct impression of her beauty. The source of this impression is the delicacy and charm with which the lines themselves move.

Had this poet's subject been a farewell to the world and to beautiful women, the meter and rhythm of the poem would indeed have been misplaced, for style must always complement subject. But to be sure that the manner and matter of his poem are in agreement, the poet must do much more than decide which of the possible metrical forms is the best one for his subject. He comes to the medium of poetry in order to make available to us an experience that he has had or imagined. The value of what he tells us about this experience will depend greatly on his ability to expose us to the qualities that made his experience unique. If he is able to convey only the most general aspects of his experience, if we come away from his poem with a sense that we've heard it all before and in almost precisely the same way, his poem will deserve only our most general attention. And yet if his poem becomes too particular there is a good chance that it will be inaccessible to us. Now every experience is unique—so much so that it is impossible for a second person to know precisely what another has experienced. Thus, what a poet knows and feels about his subject will in the last analysis remain private. But what he says about it and the way he says it should not. For any poem to have relevance for us we must have had, or at least be able to imagine, our own particular, private experiences with the kind of subject the poem presents. When we give our attention to the poem, we answer the poet's request that we apply what we know firsthand about the subject to a detailed understanding of what the same subject was for him. Meter and rhythm are tremendously important in promoting this understanding.

Throughout this chapter I have emphasized the distinction

between meter and rhythm, and meter has taken on the characteristics of some villainous fraud whose only impulse is to impose himself between your ear and the way the poem really sounds. But this is not entirely true. Although you should continue to recognize the distinction between meter and rhythm, accent and stress, and although you should remain very much aware of how limiting the terminology of meter can be when you are trying to describe how a poem sounds, you should at the same time see that if you can scan a poem you will have provided yourself with an important clue to what that poem is very particularly about. Just as you and the poet share in common the general understanding of what certain experiences are like, so, too, you can share the general expectation of what iambic pentameter sounds like before it is "fleshed out" with the words that present their own very particular rhythms. These rhythms function as signals. They show us how the poet responds emotionally to the material that the words themselves present. Because many of his responses are extremely subtle, we must remain very sensitive to the rhythm of the poem if we are to receive its signals. It is by seeing to it that meter creates in you certain patterns of expectation that the poet increases your sensitivity to every rhythmic feature of his poem. If you can learn to apply to individual poems the metrical terminology that I have tried to provide, you will have a standard against which you can begin to measure the uniqueness of each poem. You will have defined what the poet expects you to expect in order that you might then proceed to an insight into the precise way in which his experience differs from all others. Until you can do that much, both the highly particular rhythm of the poem and what that rhythm shows you about the poet's experience will necessarily elude you.

We are now going to return to the poem with which the chapter began, listening to it as sensitively as possible, to see if we can determine how its meter and rhythm relate to its subject. In discussing the function of meter and rhythm, one inevitably exaggerates. Please remember that the effects of all facets of poetic style are so particular that they can never be translated into concepts. The things that I will suggest about the meter and rhythm as they contribute to the meaning of our poem should thus be read with some suspicion. I do not doubt that something like what I will be suggesting does in fact operate in the poem; but for the composite effect of the poem's meter, rhythm, and meaning you must finally trust yourself.

How do we learn about our poet's subject by listening to his poem? Perhaps the best way to describe the general effect of the meter and rhythm of this poem would be to say that it imitates the impact on the poet of the natural details and memories that cause his nostalgia. If we are to know how he felt when he returned to the house, we must be able, in a sense, to return there with him. The opening lines introduce us to the countryside house he had visited years earlier.

> Under the mountain, as when first I knew
> Its low black roof and chimney creeper-twined,
> The red house stands; and yet my footsteps find,
> Vague in the walks, waste balm and feverfew.

As he would of course expect, the house is in the same place as it had been when he had first "known" it, "and yet" almost everything else about it has changed. In the first lines we encounter only very slight hints of the changes that the years have brought to the house, changes that we will see working strongly on the poet as the poem progresses. Although the first foot of the poem is a trochee, the rhythm of the first lines is fairly regular, and very slowly, perhaps only half-consciously, we begin to expect an uninterrupted, alternating sequence of lightly and heavily stressed syllables. But in line 4, with the first reference to the decay of the house, this sequence is broken quite abruptly. Not only does the line begin with a trochee, but the unaccented syllable of its third foot—"waste"—receives extremely heavy stress. The contrast between this line and the earlier ones qualifies what the words of the lines tell us. It emphasizes, however subtly, the way the signs of decay have begun to register with the poet. Notice, too, the way the rhythm relates to the syntax of the sentence following the semicolon in line 3. The poet wants to tell us what he has found, the balm and feverfew; but before he reveals their names he feels compelled to interject a description of their significance to him. Random, wild, indifferent to the will of the tenants who had earlier preserved the walks, these herbs are evidence, to the poet and to us, of the temporal gap that is the source of his sadness.

But no change that the house has undergone with the years impresses the poet more strongly than the vivid realization that its tenants are gone.

> But they are gone: no soft-eyed sisters trip
> Across the porch or lintels; where, behind,
> The mother sat, sat knitting with pursed lip.

We are not told where they have gone or even whether they are dead or alive. It may be that the poet has retained contact with the whole family, and that the nostalgia he now experiences is simply a product of his awareness of the mutability of all things. Or his return to the house might be a more painful reminder of the death of a member, or members, of this family. Our speculation in this matter isn't necessarily relevant to an understanding of what we're being told. What we must recognize is the intensity with which the poet feels the absence of human contact. His sense of loss is undoubtedly greatly strengthened because the sisters, in this setting, had been very special people for him. And yet I think it is enough for us to know not the precise nature of the loss but rather just how that loss has affected him. We are dependent upon the rhythm of the lines for much of what we know about this effect. The first two feet of line 5 are direct and authoritative. The people are gone; the rhythmic rigidity of the two feet which tell us that they are gone stresses the finality of their absence. But notice what happens to the rhythm when the poet begins to reconstruct his memory of the sisters and their mother. Very quickly, the rhythm becomes imitative of the actions that are described; and as it does so we are acquainted with these absent tenants in so immediate a way that we are better able to appreciate the poet's own sense of loss. He recreates for us only one of many memories he has of the "soft-eyed" girls: These "sisters trip/ Across" from one line to another, while behind them their mother knits. Notice how the repetition of "sat" after the caesura and the heavily stressed though unaccented "pursed" help to reflect the stolidity of the mother and render her alive for us.

With the conclusion of the memory, the poet confronts the present scene in its vacant inactivity.

> The house stands vacant in its green recess,
> Absent of beauty as a broken heart.
> The wild rain enters, and the sunset wind
> Sighs in the chambers of their loveliness
> Or shakes the pane—and in the silent noons

> The glass falls from the window, part by part,
> And ringeth faintly in the grassy stones.

Lines 8 and 9 return to a more regular movement. The contrasting lightness of their caesuras after those of the previous lines suggests the uninterrupted decay that has occurred in the absence of the poet's friends. These two lines are as direct a statement of the poet's response as we are to find in the poem. Although we have been shown in the preceding lines that the house is unmistakably vacant in that the "beauty" of the girls has been reduced to a memory, we have been able only to assume how strongly these changes have affected the poet. When we encounter the reference to a broken heart in line 9, we will at least be tempted to ask—though of course we do not know—if the broken heart is the poet's own. Except for the reminder of the "loveliness" of the girls in line 11, the last five lines of the poem are devoted exclusively to a description of the house as it is now, interacting with the natural elements. As the poet represents the disintegration of the house by recording how it is continually becoming more like the landscape itself, it becomes difficult to talk about his own response to the scene. I think we needn't question that he is indeed saddened by the absence of the girls. But at the same time, this sadness does not seem totally to overwhelm his ability to find beauty in the present scene.

Now some kind of fusion of sadness and beauty is clearly the essense of nostalgia, and we don't have to read the poem with any great care to discover that it deals with nostalgia. But the more carefully we read the poem, the more we recognize how much care the poet has taken so that we might know what made his particular nostalgic experience unique. As he imagines the violence of the rain, he imitates its action in the three successive heavily stressed syllables. And in the following line, the movement of the "sunset wind" is evoked as the line skips rapidly through seven syllables that are lightly stressed. In the second foot of line 13, a trochee has been substituted to imitate the falling of the glass. And the heavy caesura in that line, followed by the parenthetical phrase, slows the poem down and prepares for the final line, in which the poet wants to suggest the quiet unobtrusiveness of the entire scene. Even the rhyme scheme functions imitatively. Because the poem is fourteen lines of iambic pentameter, we might expect it to employ one of several rhyme schemes traditionally found in sonnets; and indeed the first half of the poem seems to be headed in that direction. After the very regular *abba* scheme has been established in the first four lines, the *cdc* that follows in the next three is still regular enough, provided that the anticipated *d* rhyme follows in line 8. But it does not. As we enter the description of the house in its present state of decay, the poet employs a highly irregular *efdegf* scheme through line 13 and ends on the only imperfect rhyme ("stones" and "noons") in the poem. Once he has hinted that he would use a regular rhyme scheme, the subsequent disintegration of the scheme very effectively evokes the disintegration of the house itself.

I remind you again that to talk about the rhythm of the poem as we have done is indeed to exaggerate the kind of emotional responses which its sound and meaning prompt in us. Still, had the poet not aroused in us certain metrical expectations, had he presented us instead with a strict prose account of his return to the house, we would have been even more limited than we now are in knowing precisely what the sound of his words is supposed to evoke. For once we have recognized that his poem is written in iambic pentameter, we have a common ground against which the rhythm of the poem can record its subtle emotional tremors. Meter and rhythm have thus combined to provide us with a more thorough, more precise insight into the nature of another's experience than would have been possible without them.

But if all this is true, if meter does in fact enable a poet to convey certain nuances that he might not be able to convey in prose, what kinds of things does the writer of free verse do to deserve the title of poet? Since free verse by its very nature denies those expectations that "bound" verse creates in us, is there anything, finally, that distinguishes free verse from prose? Since its freedom involves the observance of even more rigorous disciplines than those we have noticed in metered verse, there is a vast difference between free verse and prose. Indeed, the label "free" is truly paradoxical. The poet who writes good free verse must know everything that there is to know about meter—and he must know more. For in writing free verse he deliberately avoids (1) slipping at any point into a rhythmical pattern that arouses, and subsequently satisfies, metrical expectations, and (2) repeating the rhythm of one of his lines in another. And besides preventing his lines from drifting into any recognizable pattern, he must also see to it (3) that his lines move interestingly in themselves, and (4) that their movement complements the subjects which they present.

You will remember that the first step in scanning a metered line is to divide it into feet. Until this is done it is impossible to determine the number and kinds of feet that constitute the particular metrical pattern of the poem. Now a free verse poem may contain the same number of syllables from line to line, or it may contain the same number of heavily stressed syllables from line to line. But it is dedicated to avoiding any recognizable pattern of accented syllables; as soon as it falls into an iambic, trochaic, dactylic, or anapestic pattern it ceases to be free. Since the foot is a relevant unit of measurement only for the poem that creates both accentual and syllabic expectations in the reader, it cannot apply to the free verse poem. When you attempt to determine how a line of free verse works, therefore, you do not have recourse to the consistent method of scansion that can be applied to more traditional lines. Your scansion of the free verse line will have to be based, very simply, on the rhythm of the line as a whole.

There are essentially three kinds of free verse, two of which I have already mentioned. One of the poems that we discussed in an earlier chapter is an excellent illustration of the *syllabic* kind of free verse. I will quote it again.

Old Woman

Not even in darkest August,
When the mysterious insects
Marry loudly in the black weeds,
And the woodbine, limp after rain,
In the cooled night is more fragrant,   5
Do you gather in any slight
Harvest to yourself. Deep whispers
Of slight thunder, horizons off,
May break your thin sleep, but awake
You cannot hear them. Harsh gleaner   10
Of children, grandchildren—remnants
Of nights now forever future—
Your dry, invisible shudder

Dies on this porch, where, uninflamed,   ╱◡◡╱╱╱◡╱

You dread the oncoming seasons,   ◡╱◡◡╱◡◡   15

Repose in the electric night.   ◡╱◡◡◡╱◡╱

The scansion I have offered is only a vague approximation of the rhythm of the line, for I have used a notation that takes account of only two degrees of stress. But despite the fact that this kind of notation is only a distorted representation of the way the poem sounds, it at least enables me to know quite distinctly that I am not dealing with a poem written in one of the traditional metrical forms. Notice that each of the lines contains eight syllables. That fact in itself might lead you to suspect that the poem is written in tetrameter; but you would discover very soon that the poem is a very irregular tetrameter indeed. The line that comes the closest to an iambic movement is the tenth. Several other lines (1, 8, 9, 11, 13, 14, 15, and 16) contain what might be scanned as two iambs in succession. But the movement of the adjoining syllables of these lines helps to render them free. Nor is the rhythm of one line repeated in another until late in the poem (lines 11, 13, and 15). The rhythm of the poem as a whole has skillfully avoided the kinds of patterns that might have ruined it. This much you can decide by scanning the poem, but having done so will not tell you that the poem is an excellent piece of free verse. I suggest to you that it is.

A second kind of free verse, which I illustrate below, is usually called *accentual* free verse. The rhythm of the poem is such that each line contains two heavily stressed syllables.

The Last Distances

The first distances   ◡╱╱◡◡

Were cultivated, proper.   ◡╱◡◡◡╱◡

With them I watched you for   ╱◡◡╱◡◡

Fine difference,   ╱╱◡◡

And there was none. Now,   ◡◡◡╱╱   5

Inebriate with lesion,   ◡╱◡◡◡╱◡

I ignore, as I can,   ⌣⌣/⌣⌣/
The subtleties of withdrawal.   ⌣/⌣⌣⌣⌣/

It is no longer careful,   ⌣⌣⌣/⌣/⌣
This making you a stranger.   ⌣/⌣⌣⌣/⌣   10

The number of syllables from line to line is not constant, nor do any traditional metrical patterns suggest themselves as possible norms for the poem.

The final kind of free verse is perhaps the most common. If it can be said to have any controlling principle, it would have to be that the syntactical unit tends to determine the length of most of the lines. In the poem below, notice that the number of syllables and the number of heavily stressed syllables vary from line to line but that the natural rhythm of the sentences conforms loosely to the length of the lines.

Thinking of the Oregon Rains

Wishing seasons through this haze,   /⌣/⌣⌣⌣/
I imagine a grand   ⌣⌣/⌣⌣/
Preponderance of water: ⌣/⌣⌣⌣⌣/⌣
Scotch broom and fern bowing   //⌣//⌣
Heavily toward the first fall run,   /⌣⌣⌣⌣///   5
Whorled gutters   //⌣
And their limber bark-flakes,   ⌣⌣/⌣/⌣
Steam rising from the road,   //⌣⌣⌣/
And from the chimneys,   ⌣⌣⌣/⌣
Wisps of still another gray.   /⌣/⌣/⌣/   10
What are my sins in all this weather?   /⌣⌣/⌣//⌣
Oblique remonstrances whip   ⌣/⌣/⌣⌣/
Windward into rain,   /⌣⌣⌣/
Fear settles into sounds,   //⌣⌣⌣/
As death, driest of rain forests,   ⌣//⌣⌣/⌣⌣   15
Steals nothing of the velvet dampness.   /⌣⌣⌣/⌣/⌣
And staying these metaphors of change—   ⌣/⌣//⌣⌣⌣/
Only the remembrances—   /⌣⌣⌣/⌣⌣
Remembrances   ⌣/⌣⌣

Of earlier severance from evil,   ◡◡◡◡◡◡◡ 20
Of stasis, remorseless good,   ◡◡◡◡◡◡
And of the loneliness therewith.   ◡◡◡◡◡◡◡

There are some run-on lines within separate syntactical units: "grand/ Preponderance," "bowing/ Heavily," "whip/ Windward"; but by far the greater proportion of the lines are divided according to the rhythms of the sentences themselves. It is with this kind of free verse, obviously, that we come the closest to prose. In the last analysis, the free verse that observes neither a constant number of syllables nor a constant number of heavily stressed syllables in each line can be distinguished from prose only by the care that the poet has taken with his rhythms.

Your most private response to any poem is the way its sound registers with you. Of poetry's three qualities—reference, relationship, and sound—it is sound that least represents concepts or external phenomena; and in this sense it is the most closely associated with our insistently singular feelings. There will always be some apprehensible correspondence between the content and the movement of any poem that is carefully controlled. But that correspondence will always depend for its effect on the sensitivity of both your ear and your emotion.

two sonnets

Each of the last three chapters has been devoted to a single aspect of poetic style. By considering each of these aspects separately, however, we have distorted our perspective on style, for the tone of every poem—what its style says to you in its absolutely particular way—is a composite of the references, relationships, and sounds of its words. In this final chapter I want to return to the two poems that were introduced very briefly in the first; return to them and consider their separate tones by applying to them those analytical terms that seem most relevant. As you read them, try to see how their diction, organization, and meter and rhythm combine to make each poem the inimitable statement that it is.

But I would also like you to concern yourself with something that hasn't been discussed before. The three previous chapters have been essentially descriptive. I wanted to describe a few of the more basic stylistic procedures as clearly as possible, and so as illustrations I tried to choose poems that exhibit exceptional stylistic control. In order to describe how the style of each poem functioned, though, I made a normative judgment on that poem; I assumed that its style was successful. But good poems are very rare. It is a mistake to assume that the style of a poem is successful until you can see that it is. As I discuss the tone of each of these poems I will try to speak normatively as well as descriptively and attempt to show why one of the poems exhibits greater stylistic control than the other.

You will remember that the subject matter of each poem resembles that of the other in a very general way; the simplest paraphrase of either would serve for the other. In both, the poet addresses his beloved and tells her that she will win immortality in his verse. We noted one very basic stylistic difference between the two poems, however. The first centered almost exclusively on praising the lady, the second on death. I would like now to define this difference more particularly. Here, again, is the first of the poems.

> How many paltry, foolish, painted things,
> That now in coaches trouble every street,
> Shall be forgotten, whom no poet sings,
> Ere they be well wrapped in their winding-sheet?
> Where I to thee eternity shall give,   5
> When nothing else remaineth of these days,
> And queens hereafter shall be glad to live
> Upon the alms of thy superfluous praise.
> Virgins and matrons, reading these my rimes,
> Shall be so much delighted with thy story   10
> That they shall grieve they lived not in these times,
> To have seen thee, their sex's only glory:
>   So shalt thou fly above the vulgar throng,
>   Still to survive in my immortal song.

The poem employs the same kind of explicit connectives that "Church Monuments" does. Notice how many of the clauses in the first sentence are introduced with strictly grammatical agents: "How many . . . That . . . whom . . . Ere . . . Where . . . When . . . And . . . Upon . . ." Unlike "Church Monuments," though, the poem does not argue anything that requires detailed development. In terms of its structure, the poem resembles "In Time of Plague" more than any of the other poems that we have considered. Through line 5 the poet tells his lover (1) about those who won't live and (2) that she will live because of his verse. The remaining nine lines of the poem do indeed describe the kind of "eternity" his verse will give her, but the queens, virgins, and matrons are little more than extensions into the future of the "paltry, foolish, painted things" who will be forgotten while she survives.

The argument, then, is virtually static beyond line 5. But notice the explicit transition into the final couplet from the colon at the end of line 12. What the conjunction "so" presumes to tell the lady is that she has just been given some very convincing reasons for believing in the poet's powers to make her immortal. The burden that this word carries is very great; for it calls her attention, as well as ours, to the argumentative quality of the preceding lines. It asks us, in effect, to re-examine those lines—not as an illustration of the kind of fame she might possibly receive, but rather as something that is inevitable precisely because he has argued for it so capably. Unless we can concur that he has indeed argued as effectively as he seems to think he has, we must be tempted to respond to the argument itself—or to the conjunction—in a way that the poet would not approve.

But before we decide whether he has controlled his poem's organization, we must examine more particularly the way in which it interacts with the poem's diction. We are told, in diction that refers us to abstract categories, that the poet (1) will give his lady "eternity," and (2) will delight virgins and matrons with her "story"; we are told further (3) that his beloved is her "sex's only glory," and (4) that she will survive in his "immortal song." We should conclude from all of this that his lady has presumably earned all that he is willing to do for her by her extraordinary beauty, or virtue, or both. We might thus expect her beauty to be defined in diction that refers us to concrete particularities of her appearance, and her virtue to be defined in carefully controlled abstractions. But we come no closer to her, really, than the five pronouns that refer to her. With the little information that we are given concerning her, we must be more inclined to think that her beauty or virtue is totally incidental to her survival. For the diction tells us very explicitly that the grief of the virgins and matrons in not having seen her will be prompted by her in only the most indirect way: Their delight will be with her "story" rather than with those of her characteristics that her story should represent. The poem is finally not so much about the lady praised as about the act of praising itself. And since that act does not take place in the diction but is instead only alluded to, the poem does little more than celebrate itself.

But are we justified in expecting it to do more? Isn't the poet at liberty to describe, however egocentrically, what he considers to be his own very great gift for language? The poem might be no more than an introduction to a hundred sonnets that carefully define the beauty and virtue of his lady, or that argue impressively to convince her that she will not indeed be forgotten. And yet we must not overlook the fact that, if it is to succeed as a poem which celebrates the powers of the poet himself, the style of the poem must necessarily reflect these powers. The references to the lady as her "sex's only glory" and to the delight that will follow upon reading her story in his "rimes" invite us to inquire into the precise nature of her glory and her story. But the poet doesn't seem to be interested in their nature. The explicit transition into the final couplet makes us want to know *how* she will survive and not only *that* she will do so. The diction and organization thus lead us to be concerned with issues that are apparently of only incidental relevance to the poem.

We cannot excuse this poem on the basis of what the poet might have done previously or might do subsequently in other poems; for in order to respond to the poem with the same sense of celebration that the poet himself seems to feel, we must be shown that he is truly a master of his craft. Because we sense a discrepancy between his response to the subject and our own, we must conclude that he has not really controlled the tone of his poem. This lack of control is as discernible in the meter and rhythm as it is in the diction and organization.

The meter of the sonnet is iambic pentameter, and the rhyme scheme is a very regular *ababcdcdefefgg*. The lines are consistently end-stopped, and with only two exceptions the caesurae come after the fourth or fifth syllable and are of fairly consistent duration from line to line. The exceptions are lines 6 and 10, where the caesurae follow the seventh syllable. There are only five noticeable rhythmic features in the poem, and two of these—the trochees that are substituted in the first feet of lines 9, 13, and 14—are so common in iambic pentameter that they do not elicit any extensive emotional response from us. Because the rhythm corresponds so closely to the meter throughout most of the poem, however, the other two rhythmic irregularities evoke rather intense responses. The first of these occurs in line 4:

Ĕre théy | bĕ weĺl | wrápped ĭn | thĕir wínd | ĭng-shéet?

The substitution of a trochee in the third foot of an iambic pentameter line is so rare that its effect is always violent, provided that it occurs, as it does in this case, within a very regular rhythmical context. But is such violence appropriate here? Admittedly, the line refers us very specifically to the preparations for burial of the "paltry, foolish, painted things," and the implications of death can certainly be considered violent. But the effect of this line is neutralized, two lines later, with a calm, more regularly cadenced, and almost gratuitous reference to death: "When nothing else remaineth of these days." Whatever may have motivated this shift in tone from line 4 to line 6 remains obscure, and we are thus unable to respond as the poet would like us to.

The other rhythmical feature that attracts our attention seems even more out of place within the context of the poem. Although line 12 concludes with an unstressed extrametrical syllable, it is regular enough metrically:

Tŏ háve | sĕen thée, | thĕir séx | 's ŏn | lў glŏr | ў

But rhythmically the unstressed syllable of the second foot is much more heavily stressed than the preceding syllable, despite the fact that that syllable is, within its own foot, accented. In terms of stress alone, the first four syllables of the line register in a progressively ascending order,

1   2   3   4
To have seen thee,

and their effect is made even greater by (1) the repetition of the vowel sounds in the third and fourth syllables and (2) the relatively lengthy caesura that tends to set the syllables apart from the rest of

the poem. What troubles me about the emotional force that is
generated by the sound of these syllables is that they evoke the lady,
her "sex's only glory," and only divert our response the more from
what we must finally decide is the poet's primary concern: the
certain immortality of his own poetry.

It is only fair to the preceding sonnet to say that I have
exaggerated its faults, and that it is hardly the worst sonnet that I
might have chosen to contrast with the one that follows. Nor is this
next one the best of all possible sonnets. Nevertheless, it does exhibit
greater stylistic control than the one we have just examined.

> Like as the waves make towards the pebbled shore,
> So do our minutes hasten to their end,
> Each changing place with that which goes before,
> In sequent toil all forwards do contend.
> Nativity, once in the main of light,   5
> Crawls to maturity, wherewith being crowned,
> Crooked eclipses 'gainst his glory fight,
> And Time that gave doth now his gift confound.
> Time doth transfix the flourish set on youth
> And delves the parallels in beauty's brow,   10
> Feeds on the rarities of nature's truth,
> And nothing stands but for his scythe to mow.
>   And yet to times in hope my verse shall stand,
>   Praising thy worth, despite his cruel hand.

Although it too is addressed directly to the poet's beloved, this
sonnet has even less to do with the subject of love than did the other.
Every line here refers in some form to the transiency of all mortal
things. The diction of the poem is almost exclusively analogical, and
it is handled well. The figurative level of the separate analogies
remains consistent throughout. While the concrete referents change
from sentence to sentence and sometimes even from line to line, their
abstract counterpart—Time—does not. As a result, the relationships
between the various parts of the poem are scarcely less static than
those of the other sonnet. But the structure of this poem is controlled in a way that makes it seem distinctly appropriate to the
subject. The meter and rhythm are also skillfully controlled.

The first two lines are a simile that explicitly equates the concrete action of the waves on the shore with the more abstract concept of "our minutes" hastening "to their end." Line 3 defines the simile more particularly. Notice that each of these lines, as well as the fourth, is a separate clause, and that each is prefaced with an explicit grammatical agent: "Like . . . So . . . Each . . . In . . ." Although they are less noticeable, similarly explicit transitions are at work in lines 5 through 8. As it is throughout the poem, Time is the figurative level of the diction in these lines; but there are also three literal levels. The first is a personification of the temporal stages of birth and maturity, in which the former is characterized as crawling, the latter as being crowned. The second literal level refers us to light and darkness: "the main of light" and "glory" as opposed to "crooked eclipses." These two literal levels are then subsumed, in line 8, under the personification of Time as one who gives and takes away. Nativity and maturity are now seen as agents of Time himself, and the temporal progression of an individual from birth and light through the prime of life to death and darkness is conceived of as taking place under the sponsorship of a not too benevolent overseer. Much of the success of these lines must be attributed to the explicit but unobtrusive connectives that establish the sequential relationship between the literal details: "*once* in the main of light, . . ." "*wherewith* being crowned, . . ." "and Time that gave doth *now* his gift confound."

There is a single literal level in the analogical diction of lines 9 through 12. Each of these lines relates to the other three in terms of the part it plays in personifying Time as a harvester of all things. As a harvester his primary role is that of a scytheman, who is busy transfixing, delving, and leveling youth, beauty, and everything. But secondarily, and more insidiously, Time "feeds" upon the best of what he harvests. The transition into the final couplet explicitly reverses the direction of the poem. Line 12 has told us that "nothing stands" except to be cut down by Time's scythe, "and yet" the poet tells us in the line immediately following that his verse "shall stand." As with the other sonnet, we seem to be dealing with a poet who is more interested in the act of praising than in the subject praised, for the only reference to his lady comes in the very brief apostrophe that begins the final line; and there is the suggestion that the real "worth" of the lady herself will have only the most minor influence on the survival of his verse. Because he has succeeded in defining the slow, steady, and absolute power of time in the first twelve lines, and because his interest in his lady is so limited, his subsequent claim that his own verse "shall stand" might make the sonnet appear even more egocentric than the one we discussed previously. Perhaps this claim obligates him to prove that his language is more energetic than time itself.

But what is the tone of his claim? Is it in fact so strenuously proud?

> And yet to times in hope my verse shall stand,
> Praising thy worth, despite his cruel hand.

The two most important stylistic features of the couplet are the words "in hope" and the syntax of the sentence. "Times in hope" denotes, very simply, times yet to come. But the connotations of the word "hope" drastically qualify the tone of the entire line. Indeed, we are almost tempted to read the words "in hope" as a parenthetical plea that his verse be permitted to "stand." The organization of the sentence functions in such a way that it, too, qualifies the poet's claim. The poem concludes neither with the claim itself nor with the reference to the lady. Instead, the final clause refers us directly to the first twelve lines, the subject and tone of which we had only temporarily been allowed to forget. It is the "cruel hand" of Time that brings the poem to a close, and it functions structurally to remind us of the activities of Time as scytheman in lines 9 through 12, and as giver and taker in lines 5 through 8. There is thus a sense in which the couplet invites us to question the credibility of the poet's claim that his verse shall stand.

The poet's preoccupation with time and death is emphasized by the quantitative disproportion between the many lines describing the powers of time and the line and a half describing his own. But then why the claim for his verse in the thirteenth line? Wouldn't the tone of the poem be more controlled if he had not caused us to speculate with him on the stability of his verse? The point is that such speculation is an emotional corollary of his melancholy. In his role as creator he cannot, as can God, influence the natural order. The poet's mortality is inevitable. But no less inevitable, really, is his need to resist the leveling power of time. He has not deluded himself—nor indeed does he seem to be trying to delude us—into believing that artifice takes precedence over nature.

The meter and rhythm of the poem subtly underscore both his recognition of the absolute power of time and his corresponding hope that something of his own—particularly his praise of his beloved—might accede to timelessness. In the most general sense, the metrical structure of this sonnet is identical with the last: fourteen lines of iambic pentameter which are rhymed *ababcdcdefefgg*. But here the resemblance ends. Whereas there were only three lines in the other sonnet that included substitutions, there are only four in the present sonnet that do not. Lines 1, 2, 3, 6, 7, 9, 11, and 14 all begin with trochees. Substitutions of trochees for iambs also occur in the third feet of lines 1, 5, and 10. It is only in the fourth, eighth, twelfth, and thirteenth lines that rhythm conforms closely to meter. Consider the content of lines 4, 8, and 12 as it relates to their sound. Each line is the concluding clause of its sentence; and, when contrasted with the preceding lines of its respective sentence, each implies the finality of death. And so we have:

> Like as the waves make towards the pebbled shore,
> So do our minutes hasten to their end,
> Each changing place with that which goes before,
> In sequent toil all forwards do contend.

In this context the word "forwards" ultimately refers to death, despite its rather beguilingly positive nuances of progress or advancement. Similarly:

> Nativity, once in the main of light
> Crawls to maturity, wherewith being crowned,
> Crooked eclipses 'gainst his glory fight,
> And Time that gave doth now his gift confound.

In the confounding of the "gift," the process from birth is concluded; and death is realized. Again:

> Time doth transfix the flourish set on youth
> And delves the parallels in beauty's brow,
> Feeds on the rarities of nature's truth,
> And nothing stands but for his scythe to mow.

While youth and beauty persist there is life. It is only when "nothing stands" that the finality implicit in time is realized. With each sentence, the substitutions in the first three lines reflect the varied, active pace that is life in time. The contrasting regularity of the fourth line evokes the uninterrupted evenness of death. Notice that the caesurae of these lines conform very closely to one another both in position and duration:

> In sequent toil‖all forwards do contend . . .

> And Time that gave‖doth now his gift confound . . .

> And nothing stands‖but for his scythe to mow . . .

When they are considered in conjunction with meaning, then, the meter and rhythm of the first twelve lines lead us to associate the most regular rhythms with death. But the rhythm of line 13 is also noticeably regular. Why? As a living poet actively engaged in writing verse and praising the worth of his lady, shouldn't he contrast the rhythm of this line vigorously with those lines that have come to represent death?

> And yet to times in hope my verse shall stand . . .

I think the answer is that the rhythm of line 13 corresponds more closely with the "dead" than with the "living" lines because (1) it is his melancholy that has so intensely prompted his concern for fame and (2) he is unable to deceive himself into believing it more inevitable that his art will bring him posthumous fame than that death itself will make its claim on him. What is ostensibly a logic in the transition "And yet" is in fact a highly associative and illogical coupling of the melancholy and the intimately related need to be rid of it. But in what other way might that transition be made? Thus a careful examination of the tone of the poem reveals to us that his claim for his verse is much less proud than the similar claim in the other sonnet.

If we are to decide, as I think we must, that the tone of the present sonnet is the more controlled, our judgment should not be based on the relative humility that each poet demonstrates. The tone of the second sonnet is successful because the precise nature of the poet's humility is apprehensible to us—his humility is realized within the poem. The tone of the first sonnet is comparatively unsuccessful because the more intensely we read it in search of evidence that the poet has earned the pride which he asserts, the more certain we become that we cannot apprehend the nature of that pride—it remains unrealized within the poem. His poem tells us only *that* he is proud, and we are left wanting to know why.

Judgments of this kind must always wait upon a consideration of all the stylistic elements of the poem as they interact with one another to constitute tone. In this book I have sorted out each of these elements so that you might be able to talk with some particularity and confidence about the nature of poetic style. Your final response to any poem, however, will be one that ignores the analytic separation between these elements and experiences them instead as one; for when you read a poem as sensitively as you can, reference is relationship, relationship is reference, and sound is both.

index

Abstract, 10
Accent, 50
Accentual free verse, 70–71
Analogy, 19–25, 78–79
Anapest, 51
Apostrophe, 79
Apposition, 11–12
Article, 15–16
Association, 35

"Blueflags," 14–17, 19, 21

Cesura, 57, 66, 67, 76, 77, 82
"Church Monuments," 30–33, 46,
    74
Concrete, 10
Conjunction, 15–16, 75
Connotation, 12, 80, 81

Consonant sounds, 50
Couplet, 40, 80

Dactyl, 51
Declarative, 16, 32
Decorum, 41
Denotation, 12, 81
Dimeter, 52
Duration, 50
"During Wind and Rain," 33–36,
    38, 43, 46

End-stopped line, 61, 76
Explicit analogy, 19–21, 78–79
Explicit transition, 29–34, 40, 46–47,
    74–75, 79
External, 11
Extrametrical syllable, 53

85

Feminine ending, 53, 62, 77
Figurative, 23–25, 78–79
Foot, 50
Fourteener, 52
Free verse, 68–72

"Gascoigne's Lullaby," 60–63
Grammatical agents, 9–10, 15–16, 74, 79

Hexameter, 52
"How many paltry, foolish, painted things, . . ." 5–7, 74–83

Iamb, 51
Imperative, 29, 32
Imperfect rhyme, 68
Implicit analogy, 22–25
Implicit transition, 33–47, 82
Internal, 11
"In Time of Plague," 28–30, 32, 33, 34, 35, 46, 75
"In whose will is our peace?" 10–14, 15, 16, 17, 18–19, 21

"The Last Distances," 70–71
"Like as the waves make towards the pebbled shore, . . ." 5–7, 78–83
Literal, 25–35, 79

Metaphor, 23
Mixed meters, 53
Monometer, 52
"The Most of It," 36–39, 43, 46

"The Night Piece, to Julia," 62–63

Objective, 39
"Old Woman," 22–25, 69–70
"On My First Son," 39–42, 46

Paraphrase, 6, 31
Pentameter, 52
Personification, 43, 79
Pitch, 50
Preposition, 15–16
Punctuation, 58

Reference, 9
Refrain, 29–30, 33
Repetition, 16, 20, 29
Rhyme, 61, 63, 67–68, 76, 81
Run-on line, 58, 72

Scansion, 50
Secondary pause, 57
Simile, 79
Sonnet, 67–68, 73ff.
Spatial organization, 36–39
Stress, 50
Subjective, 39
Substitution, 55, 63, 76–77, 81
Syllabic free verse, 69–70
Syntax, 16, 58–59, 65, 71–72, 80

Temporal organization, 35–36, 43–46
Tetrameter, 52
"The earth with thunder torn, with fire blasted, . . ." 18–21, 22, 23, 25
"Thinking of the Oregon Rains," 71–72
"This Is Just to Say," 2–4
"To Autumn," 42–46
Transition, 16–17, 28
Trimeter, 52
Trochee, 51

"Under the mountain, as when first I knew . . ." 49–52, 54–59, 65–68

Variation, 55
Vowel sounds, 50